Managing
Teams

Other titles in the Briefcase Series include:

Motivating Employees by Anne Bruce
and James S. Pepitone

Hiring Great People by Kevin C. Klinvex,
Matthew S. O'Connell, and Christopher P. Klinvex

Effective Coaching by Marshall J. Cook

Performance Management by Robert Bacal

The Manager's Guide to Business Writing
by Suzanne D. Sparks

Managing Teams

Lawrence Holpp

McGraw-Hill

New York San Francisco Washington, D.C. Auckland Bogotá
Caracas Lisbon London Madrid Mexico City Milan
Montreal New Delhi San Juan Singapore
Sydney Tokyo Toronto

McGraw-Hill

*A Division of The **McGraw·Hill** Companies*

2 3 4 5 6 7 8 9 0 DOC/DOC 9 0 3 2 1 0 9

ISBN 0-07-071865-2

Library of Congress Cataloging-in-Publication Data

Holpp, Lawrence
   Managing Teams / Lawrence Holpp
      p. cm
   A Briefcase Book
   ISBN 0-07-071865-2
   HD66.H65 1999
   658.4/02 21
   98041553
   Subject: Teams in the Workplace — Management

This is a CWL Publishing Enterprises Book, *developed and produced for McGraw-Hill by* CWL Publishing Enterprises, *John A. Woods, President. For more information, contact CWL Publishing Enterprises, 3010 Irvington Way, Madison, WI 53713-3414, www.execpc.com/cwlpubent. Robert Magnan served as editor. For McGraw-Hill, the sponsoring editor was Catherine Schwent, the publisher was Jeffrey Krames, the editing supervisor was Frank Kotowski, Jr., and the production supervisor was Suzanne W. B. Rapcavage.*

Printed and bound by R. R. Donnelley & Sons Company.

This publication is designed to provide accurate and authoritative information in regard to the subject matter covered. It is sold with the understanding that neither the author nor the publisher is engaged in rendering legal, accounting, or other professional service. If legal advice or other expert assistance is required, the services of a competent professional person should be sought.
> *—From a Declaration of Principles jointly adopted by a Committee of the American Bar Association and a Committee of Publishers*

Contents

Preface   ix

1. Questions to Ask Before Starting Teams   1
What Are Teams?   3
The Five Ps in Team   3
Why Do You Want Teams?   8
Where Do You Plan to Implement Teams?   9
What Do You Expect from Teams?   11
What Roles Are Crucial to the Team Process?   13
How Will You Evaluate Individuals Versus Teams?   14
How Will You Compensate Teams?   16
What Resources Will You Budget for
     Training and Development?   16
What's the Organizational Impact of Teams and
     How Can You Manage It?   17
Manager's Checklist for Chapter 1   18

2. Creating the Culture for Teamwork   19
Why Teams Make Sense for Business Today   22
Moving from Traditional to Self-Directed Teams   23
How Do You Know You're Ready for
     Empowerment and Teams?   24
Determining Your Readiness for Teams   28
Manager's Checklist for Chapter 2   30

3. Teams and Business Strategy   31
How Can You Determine if Teams Are
     Right for Your Business?   31

Some Business Reasons for Teams   34
Is the Work Appropriate for Teams?   37
Are Your People Ready for Teams?   39
A Question More Important than Answers   40
Manager's Checklist for Chapter 3   42

4. **Why Organizations Have Problems with Teams**   **43**
Five Major Potholes   45
Filling the Potholes   54
The Team Development Checklist   57
A Team Development Strategy   57
Manager's Checklist for Chapter 4   66

5. **Vision, Values, Mission, and Strategy**   **67**
Begin with a Vision ... and Values   68
Missions Mean Muscles   73
Strategy: Planning for Success   74
Lead the Way ... from Within   79
Manager's Checklist for Chapter 5   80

6. **Team Dynamics**   **81**
How Teams Are Supposed to Develop   81
How Teams Really Develop   82
How to Identify, Diagnose, and Treat
    Common Team Problems   82
Manager's Checklist for Chapter 6   99

7. **New Roles for Leaders of
   High-Performance Work Groups**   **100**
The Six Roles of a Successful Manager   101
The Seven Bases of Power   103
Leadership Self-Analysis   104
Manager's Checklist for Chapter 7   108

8. **Conducting Team Meetings**   **109**
The Problem with Meetings ...   109
Meetings and Roles   110
Guidelines for Effective Team Meetings   113

Handling Common Team Meeting Problems   117
What You Should Do as Manager   120
Problem-Solving Techniques for Meetings   120
Manager's Checklist for Chapter 8   128

9. Coaching Teams and Team Members   **129**
The Basics of Coaching   130
Job Performance   131
Developing Team Players   136
Developing Leaders   137
Coaching from a Distance   144
Players as Coaches   146
Recognition   146
Coaching by Example   148
Manager's Checklist for Chapter 9   149

10. Coping with Conflicts and Changes   **150**
Resolving Conflicts   150
Direct Dealing   151
Reducing Conflicts   159
Coping with Changes   165
Manager's Checklist for Chapter 10   169

11. Applied Empowerment   **170**
Problems with Empowerment   170
A Simpler Approach   174
Manager's Checklist for Chapter 11   187

12. Evaluating Your Team   **188**
What Are Your Team Performance Problems?   188
How Effective Is Your Team?   190
How Good Are the Members of the Team?   192
How Else Can You Evaluate Your Team?   194
Manager's Checklist for Chapter 12   196

Index   **197**

Preface

Some years ago, my boss and I took a long ride from Pittsburgh to Cleveland to meet with a contingent of management and union representatives at a major steel manufacturer. The topic was how to introduce teams into a new cold-rolled steel plant they had just completed. They had never had teams before, they had a history of labor-management difficulties dating back generations, and they were still in receivership, with profitability only a dream.

Though the conditions were not ideally suited to a positive first encounter, the meeting went worse than I could have imagined. It was held in a conference room with a long table. There was not enough room for me and my flip charts and transparencies. The union reps lined one side of the table. The engineer-managers sat on the other side.

The new plant manager took us on a blueprint tour of the new plant from a wall chart at the back of the room, which was covered with schematics. He walked us from station to station along the new line, describing with pride how few operators were needed at each station and how they wouldn't have to interact with each other but could be assigned at the beginning of each shift and left in place until the end. He pointed with glee at the computer control center and called up images of white-coated lab technicians with two-year degrees who would control every slightest movement of the steel. From his description, it seemed like the steel was one long piece of silvery taffy, rather than a near-molten belt of iron.

In an effort to sound intelligent, I tried to punctuate the plant manager's talk with questions that sounded reasonable. He would pontificate about the duties of employees sitting in catbird seats high above the rivers of steel flowing below them and I would ask, "Well, how much time have you built in for team meetings and problem-solving?" or "How would house-keeping duties be shared among different job categories?"

Each of my interruptions he treated like a personal slight, until, exasperated, he finally shut me up, saying, "Please hold your questions until after I finish my tour." It was clear that this meeting was going to be a little more one-way than I was used to.

When the plant manager finished, he called for a break—probably so the union representatives could have a cigarette in the hall instead of in the meeting room. I tried to chat it up with a few of them, but they seemed as surly and suspicious as a herd of buffalo.

I suggested to my boss that we make a run for it during the break. But though she was reasonable and empathized with me, she reminded me that we were billing the entire day and had an obligation to hang in there to the end.

When we reconvened, I had little hope of leading a stimu-lating interactive discussion, but I was even less prepared for what did happen. As they were all taking their seats, we wait-ed a moment for the union reps to get fresh cigarettes going and for the engineers to complete what seemed like secret calculations they'd been working out on napkins in front of them. Then the plant manager leveled his steely gaze at me.

"All right," he said. "What do we do?"

"Well," I said, "let me begin with a few questions." I had prepared ten questions that I hoped would get us into long, drawn-out discussions and bring us to the end of the day. But not even my thoughtful, open questions, probing queries into the nuances of their production design, roused them from their stony silence. They were out to get the most of the per diem fee they'd paid for my time.

"We can discuss some of these things later," the plant manager said. "What we need is this," he pointed his finger emphatically at me. "We need to know how you go about starting teams."

Now I was really on the spot. It seemed to me that what they wanted to do was simply declare teams, as if they were just adding a new policy to the company employee manual. Once they did that, then they could go on to do all the other mechanical things, like having meetings and managing inventory—familiar things they felt comfortable with.

"How many teams have you decided to have?" I asked.

"We don't know," the plant manager said. "That's why you're here."

Needless to say, I felt a little antagonism in the air. It was clear that someone had told the plant manager to bring in some consultant, that he wasn't doing it out of his own deep search for meaning. It was an unfair situation, both to us and to the union reps, who continued smoking and staring down at their steel-ravaged hands.

It was a setup, though neither I nor my boss realized it. Neither management nor labor really wanted to explore teams, nor did they even have a clear picture of what they were, but both were committed to some form of cooperation and teams seemed a concrete way to go. What they needed to make them feel better was some fool of a consultant standing up and assuring them that teams were basically a no-brainer and that they were already doing just exactly what they were supposed to do. Nobody wanted to hear about the slow process of culture change, or the role of leaders, or the massive investment in training and personal development that was part of a team start-up.

When they realized they weren't going to get anything out of me otherwise, they reluctantly let me make my pitch about culture, team development, barriers, land mines, potholes, and all the other terminology I used to characterize team progress and hurdles.

But they had no taste for mysteries: they had steel to roll out. We muddled through the rest of the meeting, relying on several dozen prepared overheads and a videotape we'd brought along. But we were fooling no one. We simply didn't have the goods.

Later on, back at the office, I wrote myself a short note. In it I spelled out the kinds of things I needed and had to have to enable me to do my job. That list included:

1. A reasonable background, with several examples of empowering work strategies and some detailed knowledge about them.

2. A process for creating empowered teams that went from A to Z. I wanted a method to identify teams, articulate what they do, assign duties, train them in their new roles, and provide them with the support they needed.

3. Answers to commonly asked questions. This was a little trickier. I wanted to have a pretty good idea of the questions people would tend to ask and I wanted to be able to answer them, not glibly, but honestly and thoroughly.

4. A way to express, in understandable terms, the massive change in culture and even personality that is needed to empower individuals and help them emerge from more traditional organizational designs. I needed a way to explain what needs to happen in the hearts and minds of managers and employees alike in order to achieve the trust and respect needed to be successful in this kind of participation at work.

5. Finally, and perhaps most important, I wanted a set of tools to use to help teams, team leaders, and managers create empowerment strategies. These would have to be tools that were simple and easy to use but that didn't oversimplify a complex task.

Well, I haven't gotten all the answers I need yet, but I have gleaned a few. Success at creating and nurturing teams is only partly determined by the tools and techniques you as a consultant, either outside or inside, bring to the picture. The rest has to do with the organization, the leadership, the team members themselves, and the overall readiness of the critical success factors to work together in harmony.

What are those success factors? Mostly they have to do with planning and addressing the right questions:

- Why do we want teams?
- What are they supposed to do?
- What changes will we have to make to ensure their success?

Wherever you are on the road to teams—just starting out or well down the path—you must boldly ask and answer some tough questions. No consultant can answer these questions for you; you have to do that yourself. Saying, "I don't know" is OK—for a while. But saying, "I don't care" is not OK. These questions, if unanswered, unconsidered, will turn into problems sooner or later.

Let's start this book, then, with a little self-examination. Do you really want to get involved with teams? Have you got the stomach and the pocketbook for teams? Do teams make sense for your business? Is management committed to teams?

If you're part of a design team, work with your team to answer the questions posed in Chapter One. If you can't come up with the answers right away, don't worry—but don't forget to return to the questions before some irate team member asks it in an open forum, and you're caught unprepared. But don't give up hope.

Read on. This book will provide you with alternatives, if not answers to the questions in Chapter One. Stick with the program, and you'll soon know more than most consultants.

Special Features

The idea behind the books in the Briefcase Series is to give
you practical information written in a friendly person-to-person
style. The chapters are short, deal with tactical issues,
and include lots of examples. They also feature numerous
boxes designed to give you different types of specific information.
Here's a description of the boxes you'll find in this book.

These boxes do just what they say: give you tips and
tactics for being smart in managing the team-building
process.

These boxes provide warnings for where things could
go wrong in the team environment.

Here you'll find best practices you can use to make
the process go more smoothly.

Every subject has its special jargon and terms. These
boxes provide definitions of terms used in building
teams.

Want to know how others have successfully implemented
teams? Look for these boxes.

Here you'll find specific procedures you can follow to
facilitate the success of teams.

How can you make sure you won't make a mistake?
You can't, but these boxes will give you practical advice
on how to minimize the possibility.

Acknowledgments

This book represents the accumulation of information and practices I have learned and implemented working with many companies, and I wish to thank the many different people and companies who have given me the opportunity to help them set up successful teams.

John Woods of CWL Publishing Enterprises asked me to write it, and the final book is really a collaboration between John, his associate at CWL, Bob Magnan, and myself. I appreciate their help in the development of the final product.

Finally, I wish to thank you for choosing this book to help you in the team-building process.

About the Author

Larry Holpp has spent 25 years implementing team-based strategies in a wide variety of organizations to support total quality, worker involvement, union-management cooperation efforts, and advanced manufacturing innovations. As a consultant, Larry worked with both service and manufacturing clients and helped institute total quality programs in a dozen hospitals and self-managing teams in both manufacturing and financial services companies. He is author of *Team Turbo Training*, a series of tactical training modules published by McGraw-Hill (1999), and over twenty articles on teams, quality, and empowerment in journals such as *Training*, *The Journal for Quality and Partiticipation*, and *Training & Development*.

Questions to Ask Before Starting Teams

"**D**on't mention teams to me," said the plant manager. "They're nothin' but trouble. Trouble and expense. Trouble and expense and time. I've already got troubles, I've already got expenses, and I don't have any time."

"How can you say that?" asked the internal consultant. "Teams have shown their value in industry after industry in achieving both quality and productivity goals. You've looked at that report I sent you, haven't you?"

"Yes, but it also says that teams take years to develop. I have productivity and quality goals, all right, but we measure them in days, not years. Besides, I've listened to people at the Plant Managers Conference. Plenty of them have started teams and those who are honest about it—and there's not a whole lot of them—say that for every win there's a crash and burn. Explain that."

"It's true, you're right. But there are reasons why teams fail. Listen, we're both under a corporate mandate to make recommendations on how to introduce high-performance teams here. We've got to come up with a plan, some sort of a process. We can't just send a memo and say, 'Forget it, too much trouble.'"

This conversation between a manager and a consultant charged with exploring the team concept probably didn't actually take place. At least none of the principals will admit to it. Everyone is still paying homage to teams, teamwork, empowerment, and self-management, but the buzz is gone. In the last year alone, dozens of firms have abandoned or put the brakes on their team-development efforts for any or all of the following three main reasons:

1. Teams cost too much.
2. Teams don't provide bottom-line results quickly enough.
3. Teams are poorly understood by line managers who have to foot the bill or spend the time in meetings and training sessions that seem useless to them.

Why do companies get started with teams and then drop the effort like a hot rock at the first sign of inconvenience or trouble? There are a variety of reasons for this failure of will and vision, and many of them fall under the head-

For Example: Why Have Organizations Dropped Their Teams?

A major aerospace manufacturer developed a five-day training program to help managers of team leaders understand the dynamics of the high-performance work groups that were forming in the ranks. After two pilot sessions, program revisions, and a train-the-trainer program, the course was blessed by management but never delivered. Boxes of books and tapes now sit in a warehouse.

A national home improvement retailer decided to use teams at its new distribution center, a 500,000-square-foot facility with the latest technology. After developing a selection procedure, a leadership program for management and team leaders, and a team-training program for all new hires, it abandoned the effort when its technical systems crashed and began causing unanticipated problems.

A major insurance company was fascinated by the concept of empowered teams and had made some headway in developing them. Then market share began declining. Now, talk of teams is dead, and those who are already working in teams wonder where the support went.

ing of planning. In our work with organizations that have experimented with teams, some successfully and some not, we found that by asking and answering a few questions beforehand the probability of implementing a successful team-work process increases dramatically.

If you are contemplating teams and any kind of teamwork or empowerment strategy, here are a few questions to ask before starting the process. By answering these questions, or even just discussing them, you will begin to get a feel for the planning required before launching teams in your organization.

But let's be honest about it. If it looks to you like too much trouble and time, take the hint: You probably shouldn't do it. If you're not willing to invest the time, then it's unlikely any team initiative will succeed. But then, that's probably true for any major initiative in any organization.

What Are Teams?

That's a simple enough question, but one that's seldom asked. We all think we know intuitively what teams are, so we assume we can dispense with that question. Think again.

Sure, we all know that a team is some people doing some-thing together. We can all agree on that simple statement—and probably all disagree beyond that. That's why we've got this section in our opening chapter.

For our purposes, we could define a team as a group of people working together toward specific objectives within a defined operational sphere. And that's not a bad way to think about teams. But what does it mean in terms of successfully implementing teams? Where do we go from here?

The Five Ps in Team

Well, we propose thinking in terms of the Five Ps—purpose, place, power, plan, and people. It's a convenient way to focus on the basic areas in which you face the most important ques-tions when implementing teams in any organization.

Purpose

You should begin with the *purpose* of the teams. Why are you using teams? What do you expect them to do?

Team   We all know what this word means—"a number of individuals associated in some joint action," the dictionary informs us. So we may not think any further. That's a big mistake. A team should be defined in terms of purpose, place, power, plan, and people. If you fail to address those issues, your "team" may be little more than a group of individuals whose work is related but not coordinated in any disciplined manner.

Are they going to be natural work teams, project teams, or task-only teams? Are they going to be self-managed teams? Will they exist temporarily, then break up? Or will they last for years? Whatever the specific purpose of any team, the general purpose of all teams is that *bringing together people whose work is related and interdependent into a team allows them to work in a more collaborative manner to achieve individual, departmental, and organizational objectives.*

Place

The question of *purpose* leads naturally into the question of *place*. And that can be a big question: How do the teams fit into an organizational structure that shows only boxes, not circles and other new organizational forms? It's not just a matter of drawing a new organization chart, of course, but of adapting company thinking to a more collaborative workplace where people from many parts of the organization come together as teammates. This can play havoc with traditional organizational charts and requires rethinking how the organization is organized. When you discuss the question of *place*, you start raising some significant questions, such as the following:

- Who chooses the people to form each team?
- To whom do the teams report?
- How do we compensate teams?

After you've discussed and answered these questions of *purpose* and *place*, and any questions that arise out of your discussion, you can write a definition of your teams in terms of what you expect from them and how they'll fit into your organizational structure. Take as much care with this definition as you would if you were forming a vision or mission statement. In defining your terms, you can deliver an important message about your company's values with respect to how people work and what's expected of them.

If you're forming several teams, you might have a set definition, but different purposes. Or, if you're forming quality circles, for example, and plan on each unit in your organization having its own team, then a single, generic definition might be enough. Once you've finalized your definition in terms of *purpose* and *place*, then you can move on to the third and fourth of the Five Ps—the *power* and the *plan*.

Power

The questions you need to address with regard to *power* depend on your definition of a team and the different types of teams you might have. Your questions will also depend on characteristics of your organization—such as size, structure, and type of business. While it's difficult to cover all the issues that an organization might need to address, we can simply suggest the major concerns that should guide your thinking about the *power* component of establishing teams.

What we mean by *power* is responsibilities and authority of the team. What will be the scope of the work of each team? Will it be working on issues that affect the entire organization? Or will it focus on a certain limited area? Do you intend your teams to be primarily advisory, to make recommendations to somebody? Or do you expect your teams to take action, to

---

CAUTION!

Specify the Purpose of the Team

Take your time on discussing purpose—and be brutally honest and as specific as possible. Think of this part of the process as though you were planning to create a company.

"Hey! I've got an idea! Let's start a company!"

"To do what?"

"Aw, gee, I don't know. But it just seems like a good idea."

Funny? Yes, but pathetic. Nobody would just start a company because "it just seems like a good idea" without deciding on the purpose of that company. But managers sometimes set up teams just because "it's a good idea." And that makes it a bad idea.

Questions of Control

Team, team, who's got the team? That can be an important question when team members come from different departments—especially in an organization charged with political power games and divided by turf battles.

It's a delicate matter, but not hopeless. Your best bet might be to treat each team as if it were an outside resource, like a supplier rather than a group of employees. Managers might then be less likely to involve teams in their power plays. Of course, you should also use extra care in thinking and wording the definitions of your teams.

make things happen? Will your teams be natural (include members from one functional area or department), cross-functional (include members from different departments), or project-based? What boundaries will you set for your teams? What will be the extent of their decision-making autonomy? These are important questions to address because they directly affect the team's ability to achieve its goals.

You should set down your answers as an extension of the definition you wrote earlier. What we're talking about here is devising a sort of job description, as you might have for each position in your organization, which outlines the responsibilities and the authority for each of your teams.

Plan

The fourth P—*plan*—refers to the structure of each team. How will it assume its assigned responsibilities and handle its designated authority? In other words, who on the team will do what and how?

You may decide to leave that matter up to the members of each team. Or you may set down some guidelines. How many members would be best for each team? Will your teams each have a leader? Will that leadership position be permanent or will it rotate among the members? What responsibilities and authority will the leader have? Should you establish specific areas of responsibility and authority for other members of the group? Will the teams meet regularly? How much work will be done during meetings? How much work will members do outside of meetings, independently or in smaller teams? How much time might any member be expected to devote to the team?

> **Planning Particulars**
>
> Details, details, details .... Is the devil really in the details? Do you really need to establish every particular?
>
> Yes. No. Maybe. The right answer depends on your organizational culture. If you have very specific employee job descriptions and a thick policy manual, then you may need more detail than if your job descriptions are basically "do whatever it takes to get the job done" and the company policy manual is a thin binder gathering dust on a shelf.

Again, we can only give you an idea of the basic questions you should address. As a colleague of ours puts it, these are just "serving suggestions." How you choose to prepare your teams depends on your organization and your needs. Finally, some organizations—particularly those that are smaller or structurally less complex—may prefer to consider the *people* before moving on to the *power* and the *plan*. But it seems wiser to follow the order we're taking here, to avoid the problems that are likely to result from choosing the members of your team before you decide how you want that team to function.

People

Now for the last of our Five Ps, the *people*. This is definitely a case of "last, but certainly not least." Remember: it's the people who make the team. What you've done to establish the purpose, the place, the power, and the plan for your teams should provide the proper context for them to succeed. But it all ultimately depends on the people.

And that's where you're on your own. We don't know your people. And we don't know who's in charge of choosing the members for each team or what constraints there may be. For example, if participation on your teams is voluntary, that may shrink the size of the candidate pool. Or if the teams are cross-functional, you'll have to choose team members in terms of appropriately representing the various functions.

At this point you should encourage whoever is responsible for choosing team members to get to know the candidates better. What are the skills, knowledge, experience, and abilities of each person? More specifically, how do these resources fit your definitions of purpose, place, power, and plan for your teams?

Then, after you know all about the people in your pool, it's a matter of picking the best candidates. Doing that may not be as simple as it sounds, so what follows is some guidance.

A team is not just the five or ten best people—however you might define "best" in your particular context. A team is a mix, a combination that you hope will result in synergy.

So, the question to address here is not "Who are the best people?" but "How can we provide the best mix of resources and get the best results?" This may mean, for example, not choosing the most talented person, because she just doesn't get along with very many people. Or it may mean picking somebody who's a little short on skills and knowledge and experience, but who's got a natural ability to bring out the best in people around him.

So, that's it, the Five Ps of a good team. And now that you understand what's involved in forming teams, we come to a reality check.

Why Do You Want Teams?

That may seem like a dumb question. But we intend it as a challenge to an honest self-appraisal.

Teams, whatever their nature, are more trouble than they're worth, if they're not worth the trouble in bottom-line results. If, for example, teams are just a convenient vehicle for grouping lots of people who used to work for several supervisors down-sized out of the company and putting them under one stretched-thin manager, don't bother. But if, on the other hand, teams can truly take ownership of a work area and provide the kind of up-close process knowledge that's unavailable else-where, then full speed ahead.

Answering the question "Why do you want teams?" forces you to consider what specific business issues teams ought to be addressing. Without linking the "Why?" of teams to the needs of your business, you place their existence on shaky footing. Saying simply, "We feel teams will be good for our

business" doesn't estab-
lish a business reason for
teams. Without a strong
business purpose, teams
risk many dangers, espe-
cially the following three:

> **Synergy** The result of interactions that make the whole greater than the sum of its parts. In our context, it means that your team members are cooperating in such ways that they can accomplish more together than they would if they were all working individually.

1. Teams will waste a lot of resources going in various directions, either overly ambitious or just confused.
2. Team members will suffer from a lack of identity at crucial times because everybody needs to be motivated by a sense of purpose.
3. Teams will be among the first initiatives to suffer in the event of an economic downturn or if resources become scarce.

Justifying teams from a business perspective also forces you to consider the nature of your work, how tasks are divided, your organizational strategy and design, and how you are staffed. Teams challenge functional silos, non-communicating work groups that really should be talking to one another. Thinking about teams as a business strategy makes you rethink your business strategy as a whole. In doing so, you may find that teams are only part of a larger strategy that includes products, services, customer relationships, competitive positions, and other, broader economic issues.

Where Do You Plan to Implement Teams?

The proper answer to this question is not "here and there." Too often teams are implemented in some likely area where there are lots of people milling about doing similar things. "Hmmm," some dreamy-eyed manager says. "That looks like a team to me."

And indeed, that manager may be right. There may be the makings of a natural work team there. But, if the manager doesn't proceed carefully, he or she could lose something vital by formalizing that group of employees into a team.

Sometimes people can work closely together, benefiting

from the bond of their work. But they may not like changing that natural community into a team. It's often a question of personality, of different social tendencies, of the introvert-extrovert continuum, and so forth.

It can also be a question of your organization. Sometimes employees like forming bonds for the sake of helping each other, or drawing more motivation from their work, or just making the activities less monotonous. But those same employees might resist forming teams for any purposes established by the organization. (If that's a general feeling in your organization, you may have a lot of work to do to change that environment if you want teams to have a chance to succeed.)

But even if you have a wonderful organization and wonderful employees, will you want everybody to be part of a team? Maybe, maybe not. That's up to you.

But if you don't communicate your plan to every employee—whether they're going to be on teams or not—that's bad managing. Everyone will be on tenterhooks until you let them know how they'll be affected by a team strategy. You're causing unnecessary damage, to the employees and perhaps to the new teams.

Identify those areas and groups that have good prospects for teaming due to the nature of their work or your business requirements. Let those employees know about it and provide them with a timetable and set of expectations. Let the others know what their roles will be with respect to teams and whether they'll be asked to participate in the overall strategy.

Few organizations switch completely and easily to a team-based

---

The First Benefit of a Team

Smart Managing

"The biggest benefit of teams may come before they actually do anything." That's what a colleague once observed. And she's right.

If you plan carefully for your teams, if you really think about them, it's like you're putting together a set of small clones of your organization. With every "Why?" you're probing some very significant issues. So, even if you decide not to set up teams, you've derived some benefits from the focused, probing thinking about your organization and how things get done.

structure. And unless you take steps to prepare them, traditional power bases in functional areas can threaten the success of teams within their units and in other functional areas. Understanding their roles with respect to the teams and understanding the importance of the effort can help persuade non-teaming units to support teams and give them the helping hand they'll need to survive.

Here are a few benchmarks to help you identify likely areas for teams.

- Is the work subject to decision making best done on the spot by experienced people who deal directly with the customer?
- Is there a need for cross training and multi-skilling so that, in time, anyone can do all the jobs in the work area?
- Are your people already functioning like a team, sharing information, solving problems, raising important issues, and thinking in businesslike ways about their work?
- Do the people in your prospective team area like and respect each other?

If your answer to these questions is yes, then establishing teams in such areas will make sense. But this doesn't guarantee that teams will improve performance. It still requires a trust-based relationship between employees and management. But if this is in place, and if you answer the above questions positively, then teams are likely to succeed.

What Do You Expect from Teams?

It would be rare indeed for the seasoned business manager to implement a costly strategy, purchase a million-dollar piece of equipment, or sponsor an expensive move from one

---

Communicate Yes, it means to make known. But check your dictionary: "communicate" also means to be connected. It's generally used in that sense to talk about rooms in a building, but it's also a good way to think about people in an organization.

When you communicate, you form and build connections among your people. If you don't communicate, connections form naturally, such as company grapevines. Whatever changes you're planning or expecting, let your people know.

office to another without clearly articulating what's expected from the investment. Yet businesses enter into costly, extensive, and sometimes risky team programs without once stating in writing what results they expect.

So, what do you expect from your teams? Higher productivity? Lower costs? Improved quality? Reduced head count? Define the benefits you expect, then set targets and goals so you know if there's a payoff from your move to teams or not.

Without clear goals you'll find it difficult to assess team performance unless things go really badly or really well, both of which rarely happen over the short term. Without goals, comparing unit performance "before teams" and "after teams" is like contrasting the effectiveness of gasoline versus solar power. Both provide energy, but their start-up, maintenance, and long-term costs are very different.

What's your implementation timetable? And what are your milestones for measuring team progress toward goals?

It's often been suggested that a successful team process may take from three to five years. If you wait three to five years to decide if you have a success, you may get a nasty surprise instead.

Evaluating Team Progress in a Changing Environment

Team development takes a long time. And during the development period, many things change: membership, management, technology, and business goals. How can you measure the effectiveness of a work unit that may have turned over once or twice, is reporting to new management with new goals, and has changed its principal focus and mix of responsibilities? (Maybe only the name of the team has stayed the same!)

Whether you use standard metrics like productivity and quality, developmental indicators like degree of decision-making authority, or process measures like opinion surveys, or a combination of all three, you should plan to measure your results regularly. Identify your indicators in advance.

It doesn't really take much effort to come up with a list of things you expect from your teams during the course of one or two years. Share those expectations with your teams. Then, when the time comes to take your readings, be honest about the results, share them with the team, modify them if necessary, and establish new benchmarks based on what you learn.

What Roles Are Crucial to the Team Process?

What are the roles of leaders and facilitators? The importance of this question cannot be overstated. Your answers are critical in determining the future of your teams.

Leaders who do not have a clear vision of their role in establishing consensus, gaining commitment, developing people, and setting up the training to support those efforts will, invariably, revert to behaving like traditional first-line supervisors. Leaving the roles of manager, supervisor, or team leader to chance is an almost certain formula for ambiguity and confusion—and probable failure. Without clear roles and expectations, managers and supervisors will steer clear of the teams and hope the whole business goes away. Without written guidelines, team leaders run the gamut of behaviors from autocrat to absentee manager.

> **Dealing with Failure ... or Success**
> Smart Managing
>
> If a team fails or succeeds, it's not like when you're experimenting with a machine. We're talking about people. You can't just junk a team if it fails or buy a dozen more if it succeeds.
>
> That's another reason for setting goals and incremental targets. People don't want to fail, and a smart manager provides ways for members of a team to assess their work, so they know how they're doing. If the results are less than expected, then the manager and the team members can make adjustments. If the results surpass expectations, the manager can learn some lessons to apply to other teams.

Many organizations have taken the bold, cost-cutting step of eliminating layers of supervisors or managers and establishing teams. Nearly all have been forced to backtrack and reinstall some form of leadership. Why?

The first step in creating a team may have very little to do with the members of the team or its purpose, but a great deal

Start Smart

You might be thinking, "Hey! Working with a team is a lot like working with a new hire." And you're right ... if you provide each employee with a job description and the criteria you'll use for assessing his or her performance ... and if you allow each employee the responsibility, authority, and resources appropriate for the job ... and if you meet regularly with each employee to talk about that person's performance, making whatever adjustments you consider necessary. If so, then congratulations for being a smart manager! And you're off to a good start with your teams.

to do with how people are managed. Two issues are involved here. The first is that the managers may not be accustomed to allowing their individual employees much freedom to think and make decisions. The second is that managers tend to treat teams as if they were just groups of employees.

Changing the roles of the leader from commander to collaborator will begin to get a work group functioning like a decision-making body. As the leader becomes more skilled at developing decision-making abilities in the team, he or she can step back and assume other duties while the team adopts those responsibilities that were once the domain of the supervisor.

Leaders may not change behavior overnight, but the process of change must start with guidelines for new roles.

How Will You Evaluate Individuals Versus Teams?

Of all the traditional norms that teaming up may endanger, the one-on-one boss-subordinate relationship is perhaps the most critical and personal. Most organizations have a longstanding tradition of appraising lower-level employees not on results attained, since the employees seldom have responsibility for results, but on traits and behaviors.

These traits encompass such things as individual job skills, from typing to safety awareness, and personal characteristics, from friendliness to initiative. Some are relevant to the job, and some are not. But most focus on individuals. Case by case, it's arguable whether individual traits lead to job success. But on a team basis, the connection between individual characteristics and team results is tenuous at best.

Will you treat the team as some sort of organic whole, with members responsible for each other's performance—"One for all and all for one"? Or will you continue to emphasize individual skills and abilities? If so, who does the evaluation—the team? the team leader? management?

Perhaps the best approach is a combination of team measurements and individual appraisal. But even then, who does the appraising, the boss or the team? And how are the team members expected to react to different work styles within the team, from real stars to slow learners? Should they learn to tolerate differences ("appreciate diversity" in the current vernacular)? Or should they seek a standardized work style and allow little variation in the service of uniform output?

When the concept of becoming an empowered work group is put to employees, they often are interested in the decision-making opportunities of hiring and firing, discipline, doling out rewards, and doing appraisals on each other. In reality, very few teams ever do these things.

Xs and Ys

Theory X and **Theory Y** are the two ends of a managerial continuum developed by Douglas McGregor several decades ago. They represent the ways in which managers view workers, according to different conceptions of human nature.

A Theory X manager assumes that work is inherently unpleasant and that employees generally are lazy, avoid responsibility, and need close supervision. The Theory X manager believes that the principal motivation is money and workers must be bribed or coerced to achieve the organization's goals.

A Theory Y manager assumes that people enjoy work and that employees generally are committed to their work, exercise self-direction, seek responsibility, and show creativity and ingenuity when given the chance. The Theory Y manager believes that recognition and self-fulfillment are as important to employees as money.

Pop quiz: Which of these managerial approaches is more likely to facilitate the success of teams?

Most, instead, concentrate on doing the work and leave the personnel stuff to managers and supervisors who are paid to endure such headaches. That seems most sensible. But teams that do get involved in selecting members or giving feedback and performance management of one sort or another need substantial training, just as their supervisors and managers would have received. Good interviewing or interactive training programs can take a week or longer and require skill practices in class and on-the-job coaching and monitoring.

This is a major investment, and managers should not enter into it without considerable thought. In short, don't give teams responsibilities you are unable to train them to fully accept and handle appropriately. Otherwise, you're dooming your teams to fail—and to cause a lot of personal damage.

How Will You Compensate Teams?

Because it's sometimes a tricky issue, outside the control of direct management, the question of compensation is often left unanswered until problems arise. Although many companies bite the bullet and set up pay-for-skills or special incentive bonus programs, many fail to address compensation issues at all. The result is that team members are asked to work together, but may be offered incentives for their personal contributions. Some teams lose interest when they're asked to do more with less and then don't get rewarded for doing so.

Teams require both monetary and non-monetary rewards. Pay should be linked to achievement of objectives. On the other hand, you should liberally dispense non-monetary, symbolic awards, like cups, jackets, plaques, or dinners.

What Resources Will You Budget for Training and Development?

Be realistic in appraising the costs of launching teams. Be honest about the amount of training, meeting time, and related resources that you'll have to invest in your team effort.

All teams need to learn more about communications and problem solving, but they also need trial-and-error practice

time as they begin to assume greater self-management authority. Just as good supervisors aren't trained in a day, neither are
teams.

During the first year of its existence, a new team may
require from 5% to 10% of its salary budget just for training,
meetings, and other team-related activities. Expenses of this
magnitude can dramatically cut into expected productivity
growth and discourage managers who have not taken all the
costs into account.

Don't let budget surprises hurt your teams!

What's the Organizational Impact of Teams and How Can You Manage It?

You may not be able to answer this final question easily or perhaps at all as you start to implement teams. But it's worth
thinking about. If your
teams are to be anything
more than an experiment,
this initiative is likely to
fundamentally change
your organizational
culture.

Restructuring for
teams means that the tra-
ditional paradigms for hiring, firing, appraising,
pay, span of control, and
career development have
changed. Teams mean
you may have to rethink
and probably rewrite per-

> **Trinket Alert!**
>
> Beware of trinkets!
> Although we advise you to be gener-
> ous with non-monetary rewards, take
> care as to how you use them. Remem-
> ber: What makes them mean some-
> thing is their symbolism, the value they
> have for the recipients and for their
> fellow employees.
>
> Companies that neglect to sup-
> port and maintain that value pay the
> price. Their cups and jackets and
> plaques and dinners are valued as just
> so much plastic, cloth, wood, metal,
> and fattening food.

sonnel policies, job descriptions, performance appraisal forms,
union agreements, and many other documents.

Hierarchies have been the norm for organizations for the
last few hundred years. Teams and teamwork may very well
be the new model for many organizations for the next few hundred years. If your organization is moving in the direction of
teams, don't let it stumble along. Take an active role and you

Honesty Is the Best Policy

Smart Managing Smart managers understand human nature and they know their employees. Be honest about what you're expecting from your people and budget your time and expenses appropriately. Don't try to minimize figures in your zeal to establish teams.

In one organization, the weekly team meeting that was expected to take only one hour turned out to take two or three hours per person, as team members followed up on meeting assignments, prepared for meetings, gathered data, or learned new procedures. The moral of the story: Know what you expect and the time and resources team members will need to meet those expectations.

will avoid many pitfalls—and be able to claim some responsibility for the success of teams and teamwork.

Manager's Checklist for Chapter 1

❑ When organizations drop their teams at the first sign of trouble, it's generally because of bad planning. To improve your chances of succeeding with teams, it's important to ask and answer a few questions in advance.

❑ Define what you mean by "team." Not everybody will understand this concept in the same way. Think in terms of the Five Ps—purpose, place, power, plan, and people.

❑ Why do you want teams? Answering that question forces you to consider which specific business issues teams ought to be addressing and how your teams should be linked to the needs of your business.

❑ Define the benefits you expect from teams, then set targets and goals so you can determine the payoff, if any.

❑ How will teams affect your workplace culture, particularly the managers? Be sure they're ready for role changes.

❑ Communicate, communicate, communicate. It's the lubrication of teamwork.

Creating the Culture for Teamwork

Fred Carver decided to spend a week on the day shift rather than his regular evening shift. It took some juggling to get coverage, but it was worth it. Many of his team's problems with material consistency were coming from the day shift, and he needed to find out why.

He divided his daylight time between the Quality Assurance Lab, Purchasing, and Production Control. By Wednesday morning, it became clear that the problem was in vendor-supplied materials, not day shift procedures. So he made an appointment to visit the vendor and by noon had travel money and plane tickets from Accounting.

Most of Thursday was spent with the vendor's chemists reviewing sample control charts. It was clear that a small amount of otherwise innocuous additive had been allowed to contaminate several shipments. This accounted for the problems with material consistency.

Fred returned to work earlier than planned to work with his team leader to determine costs and waste caused by the damaged goods during the past three weeks. He wanted to be sure to get the numbers right, as that could dramatically impact their quarterly bonus. Fred's teammates were also glad to have him back on second shift since he was better than most mechanics in keeping the belts and forklifts running smoothly.

As the above slice of life suggests, members of teams assume many responsibilities. Fred Carver didn't become a traveling troubleshooter overnight. He and his teammates probably spent years getting to the point where he could visit vendors and make important decisions while continuing with his regular job driving a forklift.

Fred is a member of a *self-directed team*. This means that the team not only handles its day-to-day work, but also makes some pretty dramatic decisions about managing its own small, but important piece of the business. As we will see, self-directed teams sometimes operate with little supervision and adopt many traditional supervisor roles, including hiring, allocation of bonuses or pay increases, discipline, and even firing.

In the following slice of life we get a picture of the kinds of activities and decisions in another, very different type of team, a *high-performance work team*.

> **Key Term**
>
> **Self-directed team**
> A group of employees who are empowered to make certain decisions about their work, sometimes operating with little supervision and with authority to hire, allocate bonuses or pay increases, discipline, terminate, and take other actions traditionally handled by the supervisor.

Kate Brown and her teammates are concerned about performance, not self-management. Supervisors and managers have well-defined roles, and there are clear limits on the decision-making authority that Kate and her teammates can exercise. Unlike Fred Carver, Kate has a boss, is accountable for her time as well as her outputs on the job, and can't make management decisions without authorization and the involvement of management.

It's 8:30 a.m. on Tuesday at Eversolvent Insurance. Kate Brown is on the phone with one of her company's best agents. Together, they try to correct a billing problem that has plagued

one of their large cus-
tomers for weeks.

Later, during her busi-
ness unit meeting, Kate
describes the problem to
the team. Together they

> **High-performance work team** A group of employees who focus on improving performance, within defined parameters of responsibility and authority.

use various tools and techniques to analyze the problem and
get to its root causes. They brainstorm solutions and plan a
tentative implementation strategy. While they have no idea
what impact it will have on premium volume, loss ratios, or
other bottom-line budget measures, the proposed solution
goes a long way to satisfying some immediate customer

needs. Together the team
plans a presentation to
management to get the
go-ahead for their plan.

Kate writes up her
actions and copies her
supervisor in hopes that it
will contribute to her
favorable performance
review later this month.
She logs off her computer
at 5:00 p.m. and faces a
tough commute home.
She thinks about how nice
flex time would be, but
she accepts regular hours,

> **Teams** Small work groups (4-20 members) that have the responsibility and authority to manage many of their day-to-day job functions. In addition, team members work collaboratively to set goals, share the workload, and engage in cross training.
>
> A *self-directed team* can operate with little supervision and make important decisions, while a *high-performance work team* is focused on improving performance, within defined parameters of responsibility and authority.

like everyone else, as part of organizational policy.

The scenarios involving Fred Carver and Kate Brown show
that teams can differ considerably in the scope of their functions and in the extent of their responsibilities and authority. As
we noted in Chapter 1, when you form a team, you must
clearly define its functions, responsibilities, and authority.

The functions of a team can be roughly categorized as
technical, social, and management. The following lists should
give you a good idea of the scope of each of these three

categories. Responsibilities and authority vary: some teams responsible for a certain function may be advisory, with no real authority, while others responsible for that same function may enjoy authority that borders on autonomy.

technical functions:
- quality
- productivity
- cost containment and reduction
- equipment maintenance
- training
- assigning work duties
- workplace layout

social functions:
- holding team meetings
- scheduling vacation time
- discipline
- coaching
- team leadership
- problem solving

traditional management functions:
- budget
- personnel
- pay
- hiring and interviewing
- allocation of bonuses
- recommendation for termination

Why Teams Make Sense for Business Today

Traditionally, the concept of teamwork has been treated casually—no training, no measurement, no resources—or with a great deal of emphasis on the interpersonal issues—how we get along, style of communication, mutual interests. There's been too little focus on the real reasons for teams.

The following comparison addresses the key characteristics of work elements in the traditional workplace and the modern workplace. In the "new" workplace, the role of teams is far greater and is determined by the design of the organization itself, not by the general interest of management in teams.

Work Element	Traditional	New Workplace
Job Design	One Person/One Job	Teams and Teamwork
Organizational Structure	Tall and Narrow	Wide and Flat
Compensation	Regular Raises	Performance/Incentive Based
Decision Making	Top Down	Shared
Job Security	Lifetime	Uncertain
Supervision	Watchdog	Coordinator
Employee Relations	Adversarial	Collaborative
Quality	Controlled	Planned
Customers	Interference	Reason for Being
Training	Unplanned	Related to Core Business

Table 2-1. Teams in the traditional and new workplace

Table 2-1 compares these differences in more detail.

How Are Teams Now Different from Teams Then?

With teams, it's déjà vu all over again. Do you remember teams in industry 25 years ago? No? Well, neither do most people. But there was interest in teams then, too. As you can see in the comparison in Table 2-2, *Teams Then* were mostly concerned with teamwork. *Teams Now* are also concerned with teamwork, but they focus more on work results.

Moving from Traditional to Self-Directed Teams

It can help to think of teams as existing along a continuum rather than as conforming to any rigid definition. They vary in degree of self-direction or autonomy, with some teams handling day-to-day activities such as scheduling and work planning, while others actually hire and terminate their members and decide on salary levels and bonuses. Figure 2-1 (page 25) presents a continuum of team development, from a traditional team to a self-managing team. For most of us, the kinds of teams we're seeking to develop lie somewhere in the middle.

	Teams Then	Teams Now
Purpose	To get along better	To improve performance
Leadership	Formal leader	Rotating or project leadership
Level	Upper-level and professional	All levels
Measurement of effectiveness	How do we all feel?	How did we do?
Training	Team building groups, interpersonal skills, personal growth	Team skills, quality tools, communication skills
Tie-in to regular job duties	Little or none	New job titles and functions
Compensation	Regular raises and bonuses	Performance- and team-based
Lifespan	Temporary	Permanent
Performance Appraisal	Individual	Team
Employee relations	Quality of worklife and participatory democracy	Structural and business reasons for teams

Table 2-2. Teams then vs. teams now

How Do You Know You're Ready for Empowerment and Teams?

When we talk about assessing "readiness," we mean measuring how easy or how difficult it would be to create empowered work groups, rather than determining whether you should attempt them or not. In fact, I'd encourage any organization to try to involve its workers to a greater extent. Teams are a very good idea, but nothing is worse for an organization than a good idea put into practice badly.

That's why I advise you to consider seriously how ready you are to empower your workers through teams. To help you assess your readiness, I recommend the instrument presented at the end of this chapter.

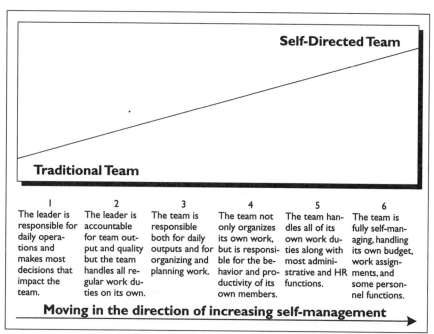

1	2	3	4	5	6
The leader is responsible for daily operations and makes most decisions that impact the team.	The leader is accountable for team output and quality but the team handles all regular work duties on its own.	The team is responsible both for daily outputs and for organizing and planning work.	The team not only organizes its own work, but is responsible for the behavior and productivity of its own members.	The team handles all of its own work duties along with most administrative and HR functions.	The team is fully self-managing, handling its own budget, work assignments, and some personnel functions.

Moving in the direction of increasing self-management

Figure 2-1. Continuum of team development

Is there a method for determining if your business is *ready* for teams? Yes.

Unfortunately, many managers don't bother with evaluating their organizations. They simply decide to "go teams." The method they adopt is closer to divine inspiration than hard work. But the approach that simply says, "Zap, you're a team" doesn't work.

How to Let a Good Idea Go Bad

In the Introduction, I mentioned my own experience of failure. Since then, I've observed many others repeat my mistake. Here's an example of how teams can fail.

At one company, a chain of high-quality restaurants, the senior managers got the itch to have their crews (teams of employees) become self-managed. They wanted the crews to begin to take over the administrative and business duties of several assistant managers who had traditionally taken care of ordering, menu planning, cleanup, personnel, and accounting.

The managers then selected one restaurant and declared it self-managing, reinforcing that pronouncement by failing to replace assistant managers who were transferred to other locations.

The result? As you might imagine, sheer chaos. Servers quit and kitchen help sat in meetings instead of cooking.

It didn't take much input from me before those managers realized that they themselves would never have tolerated what they'd done to their crews. They had unilaterally changed the conditions and the contract of employment. True, their intentions were benevolent, as they really believed in the team concept, but they failed to involve their people and they neglected to prepare for resistance to the change.

> **⚠ CAUTION!**
>
> **Go Slow**
>
> If you want teamwork, go slow. The best of intentions simply won't be enough. You need to know where you are now and where you want to go. Then you need to involve your employees in planning the steps to take. Finally, you need to anticipate problems and prepare for them.

Don't Forget: Teams Ain't Nothin' but People

Some organizations get confused about what they really want when it comes to teams and how they can "do teams." As I said, teams are a good idea, but they don't work like magic.

As a colleague was fond of reminding everybody, "Teams ain't nothin' but people." Unfortunately, a lot of managers seem to get lost in dreaming about the potential of teams and forget about the people. That was the case for the restaurant chain. It was world-class in customer service and quality, accounting methods, marketing, and sales, but the senior managers failed to exercise the same discipline when it came to planning their human resources.

Do you want to move from a *traditional* management style to a *democratic* one? Great! That's a noble goal. But don't be too confident that your employees will agree with you or that they'll be ready and able to take the plunge right away.

Do you want to know the recipe for failure for the restaurant chain? It's simple: they expected to go from traditional structure to democratic almost immediately.

In principle, nearly every kind of work environment can benefit greatly by changing from an authoritarian, traditional culture with lots of controls and clear management lines of accountability to a culture that is more participatory and stresses shared decision making. But managers who try to make that move "immediately" are expecting too much. That's how you can turn this kind of culture change, considered by many to be a "no-brainer," into a "no-winner."

No-win results come about not because managers or employees disagree with the philosophy of empowerment, but because they're just accustomed to the old management style. When managers try to change the culture, what they're really changing is the *structure*. They're moving from a highly structured culture to a culture with little structure.

The cultural dimension involved here is not in the shift from hierarchy to democracy, but in the change in structure, from high to low, from tight to loose. Maybe everybody would seem to favor a shift from hierarchy to democracy. But you simply can't assume that people who are used to working in a closely managed, highly structured environment can suddenly shift to an environment in which they're allowed and expected to make all their own decisions and assume management responsibilities and authority.

Some changes, no matter how great the eventual benefits, simply are too dramatic to make quickly. In changing the culture of a workplace, it's important to manage the change. That means making the move from a highly structured, traditional culture to a less structured, more democratic culture gradually. Divide the process into steps. Set goals for each step. At each step, check to see how the team members are adjusting to the shift and whether they appear confused or committed, reluctant or ready to move on.

Creating teams is no easier than building a new plant or introducing a major new product. In fact, it's generally harder because you're changing the way your people work, both employees and managers.

Teams Take Preparation

What have you got to lose? A lot!

When you build a plant or introduce a new product, what are you risking if you fail? Material resources. Maybe substantial, but material.

What are you risking if you fail with teams because of insufficient preparation? Your people—because you're changing the way your people work. And if you recognize that your people are your most valuable asset, that's a lot to lose.

Teams require a clearly stated objective, a set of goals, a project plan, and indicators to determine whether the implementation is proceeding as planned. Without serious planning, you're risking failure. In fact, even if you succeed, all you're likely to achieve is good teamwork within a traditional structure. Only with proper planning is it possible to develop both teamwork and teams.

Before the managers of an organization spend the time and money developing teams, they should examine the organization and make some preliminary determination of whether it's ready for teams. The following quiz will provide some answers—and raise some important questions.

Determining Your Readiness for Teams

To help you determine whether your organization is ready to empower teams, answer the questions in Table 2-3. Give yourself a score of 5 for a definite Yes, 1 for a definite No, 4 for a qualified Yes, 2 for a qualified No, and 3 for a Maybe. Then, total your scores for some indication of how ready you are.

If you score between 80 and 100, your organization will probably succeed at empowering teams. If you score between 50 and 80, you'll have to build capabilities in some of the weaker areas. If your score is below 50, or you've got 1s for a lot of the questions, you should plan to spend time examining your structure and culture or developing a vision that includes empowerment before you try to set up teams.

Questions	Yes!	Yes?	Maybe	No?	No!
1. Does management believe that employees can and should make most decisions affecting how they do their work?	5	4	3	2	1
2. Can employees suggest and implement improvements to their work without going through many levels of approval?	5	4	3	2	1
3. Are your job classifications and work rules sufficiently flexible to permit working out of scope?	5	4	3	2	1
4. Is the nature of the work in your organization more appropriate for a team-based approach than for individual effort?	5	4	3	2	1
5. Is your technology flexible enough to permit restructuring or reorganizing based on team considerations?	5	4	3	2	1
6. Is it possible to organize work so that teams can take responsibility for whole jobs rather than for component tasks?	5	4	3	2	1
7. Does the physical design of your workplace lend itself to working in teams?	5	4	3	2	1
8. Have your competitors been successful with using empowerment tactics?	5	4	3	2	1
9. Are your employees willing to organize into teams?	5	4	3	2	1
10. Do your organization's culture, vision, and values support teamwork and empowerment?	5	4	3	2	1
11. Has your organization been successful in implementing teams or other new workplace techniques?	5	4	3	2	1
12. Does your organization have a history of following through on work initiatives such as this?	5	4	3	2	1
13. Do the leaders in your organization, particularly first-line supervisors and managers, believe in teamwork and act in a manner that demonstrates that support?	5	4	3	2	1
14. Do you have enough time, money, and other resources to adequately support teams during their development?	5	4	3	2	1

Table 2-3. Assessment of readiness for teams

Questions	Yes!	Yes?	Maybe	No?	No!
15. Are you secure enough in your business to guarantee a period of relative stability during which the teams can develop without layoffs or excessive overtime?	5	4	3	2	1
16. Do you have adequate support functions like human resources, finance or accounting, and information systems that can help teams by providing information and training?	5	4	3	2	1
17. Do managers understand that developing teams is a costly and time-consuming process and are they willing and able to make a commitment in the amount of personal time they devote to it?	5	4	3	2	1
18. Does your organization have information systems capable of providing up-to-the-minute data to give teams feedback on changes and improvements in their work processes?	5	4	3	2	1
19. Do your workers have the education, job skills, and training to take greater control of their jobs? Or are you willing to make an investment in training to bring them up to speed?	5	4	3	2	1
20. Are your policies and procedures, such as compensation, flexible to adjust to new requirements teams may create?	5	4	3	2	1
Total Score					_____

Table 2-3(continued)

Manager's Checklist for Chapter 2

❑ Remember that the word "team" can mean many things in a workplace, including high-performance work team and self-directed team. So it's essential when forming a team to clearly define its functions, responsibilities, and authority.

❑ The functions of a team can be roughly categorized as technical, social, and management—how team members do their work, how they operate as a team, and how they handle managerial responsibilities.

❑ Make sure you're ready for teams and prepare appropriately according to your work environment and your employees.

Teams and Business Strategy

When teams are linked to sound business strategy, they have a solid foundation. As with any initiative, you have to be sure teams are properly funded and carefully nurtured, and you must measure and reward the results they achieve.

If managers treat teams like a business initiative, they'll be able to make the connection that links their success to the success of the team. They're then more likely to provide the support and involvement they often withhold from other efforts that seem to be only "flavor of the week" initiatives.

How Can You Determine if Teams Are Right for Your Business?

So, what circumstances would suggest that you use teams as part of your business strategy? And what possible or probable constraints should you consider when integrating teams into your strategy?

When you're asking a work group to take more responsibility for quality and productivity, then it makes good sense to use teams. You also might turn to teams if, for example, you want to reduce costs or serve your customers better. Teams can be a good idea, too, when the work requires judgment.

Or when the work consists of varied activities, particularly when they require a range of skills. In fact, the more complex the task the more appropriate it may be to assign it to teams.

Finally, if you're not sure whether you should try using teams, maybe you should look beyond your company walls. If a lot of your competitors are implementing teams, there's good reason for you to consider teams, too—not just to follow the crowd, but because your competitors are probably building their strategies on circumstances similar to yours.

Of course, whatever forces lead you to consider teams, you should also consider factors that might impede your shift to teams. Again, think and plan as carefully for as any business initiative.

Figure 3-1 summarizes the forces that drive companies to use teams and the main restraining forces.

Complex technology and the need for more extensive skills are among the driving forces behind using teams. In fact, teams are often tied to strategies intended to facilitate changes in technology or the adoption of some new process. As technology expands everywhere and approaches such as process re-engineering are dramatically transforming how we do business, companies are increasingly concerned about the competencies of their employees, especially those working in teams.

But many managers may be neglecting the skills that are crucial to the success of their teams. Although these skills aren't really new, they're certainly nontraditional for most

Driving Forces	Restraining Forces
• The competition is doing it	• Costly training
• Need to flatten the organization	• Can't find the right people
• Complex manufacturing technology	• Product demands
• Quality improvement strategies	• Union resistance
• Demanded by employees	• Unskilled managers and supervisors
• Cost improvement programs	• Don't know how to start
• Need for multi-skilled workers	• No corporate support
• Customers demand quicker service	• Short-term focus
• Perceived need to change status	• Resistance to change

Figure 3-1. Driving forces and restraining forces

employees. People who work in teams need skills convention-ally required only of managers, including the abilities to handle the following team activities:

- solve problems
- make decisions, often under pressure
- work cooperatively
- work with engineers or other process designers to improve and debug new systems and technologies

Teams may give us a great approach to working with new ways of doing business, but don't forget that in most compa-nies teams themselves are a new way of doing business. You can't simply create teams for changing systems the same way you assign individual employees to a new job task. You can't just make sure your team members have the skills necessary and then expect them to handle the task. You've got to antici-pate and meet the needs of your team members.

But how do you do that? How do you best fit together your people and your systems? Although we'll deal with this crucial question throughout this book, let's look at it briefly in the con-text of driving and restraining forces.

Socio-technical analy-sis may be the best way to ensure that any system design harmoniously melds people needs and technology. But in most instances your technology is already in place, so you're not starting from zero. It's a good idea, then, to analyze your technology and how it's used to identify any factors that could impede your use of teams.

> **Socio-technical analysis**
> **Key Term**
> The process of studying both the needs of the peo-ple and the requirements of the tech-nology to design and create a system that provides the best fit of social and technical dimensions. In other words, the machines fit the people and the people can use the machines to enhance their productivity.

The challenge is to work with the existing technology, which may not have been set up to facilitate collaboration and to make changes to minimize negative effects on your team.

Some Business Reasons for Teams

While there are many good philosophical reasons to have teams, they work best when they're driven by business demands. Don't think of teams as a concept. Instead, evaluate the potential of teams in terms of your specific business and your particular organization: What do you need to do and how do you need to do it?

In the next section of this chapter, we'll consider general business needs in terms of the following trends:

- technology
- shift in focus from function to process
- quality improvement initiatives
- reorganizing and downsizing
- advanced manufacturing technologies

Technology

Years ago, a lot of companies could compete on the basis of technology. But, as we've seen during the last decade, new technologies are readily available worldwide. Any organization can take advantage of them. Technology is no longer an assurance of a competitive edge. What matters now is how effectively people can use that technology.

Organizations are becoming more and more concerned about knowledge management, about encouraging and supporting organizational learning. In the past, managers might have talked about employees as "hired hands." Now they're increasingly engaged in tapping what's in their heads.

Moving Your Focus from Function to Process

Organizations are moving from clearly delineated functional groups—manufacturing, design, product development, marketing, sales, quality assurance, and so forth—to processes—such as product development, customer service, and operations. Teams definitely make better sense in process-focused organizations, which are more likely to be decentralized, cross-functional, leaner, faster to respond, and closer to the marketplace.

With that process focus, groups of people from various functions, with diverse specialties and backgrounds, often work together in teams. Since their work affects one another, teams make sense. Team members pool their skills, share information, and make decisions under the pressure of time while taking responsibility for outputs such as quality and cost.

As organizations shift their focus from functions to processes, many develop work groups naturally. That development may ease the transition into self-directed, self-managing teams, especially if the managers are willing to loosen their control over the groups. If not, the existence of work groups could actually impede initiatives to further empower teams.

Quality Management

Most organizations are using some kind of quality improvement initiative, whether it's total quality management, continuous quality improvement, or any of the other variations on the quality theme. During the last decade, the emphasis on quality has moved upstream, from inspecting for quality to ensuring that quality is built in at every step of the process.

But it's hard to ensure quality in a given job when that job is linked to inputs and outputs from many jobs, not all of which share goals or quality standards. As a result, quality initiatives create a climate that's conducive to teams and teamwork, particularly as employees become more committed to quality and share a sense of responsibility for doing their best. Later in this book, we'll examine the relationship between self-managing teams and total quality improvement teams.

Reorganizing and Downsizing

Very few companies can be secure and profitable if they focus on growth alone, on just doing more. Most must also try to find ways to do better. Continued success often depends on reorganization or re-engineering—and on finding and/or developing the skill sets required for the new work structures.

Initiatives to reorganize or re-engineer often involve downsizing, whether through reductions across the board and down the line or zero-basing in specific areas. The simplest approach is to eliminate jobs that don't add value. But while playing that numbers game generally reduces costs, it may not result in any real improvements—and it may stretch and strain the remaining employees. The smart complement to downsizing (or "rightsizing") is to find better ways to add value. That strategy can make the organization more efficient and more effective. And that's where teams can be so valuable, enabling organizations to do better with fewer employees.

Self-managing teams not only eliminate the role of the traditional supervisor, but also take responsibility for quality, maintenance, scheduling, ordering, and customer relations. These jobs are incorporated into teams and completely eliminated as separate functional areas. Also, team members pool their abilities and focus their energies on whichever tasks or areas need attention at any given moment, providing more capable and more flexible coverage of organizational needs.

Advanced Manufacturing Technologies

Another trend that may affect your organization is new manufacturing technologies, which include just-in-time inventory, advanced integrated design capability, statistical process control, and integrated work cells. These technologies demand better educated workers with greater knowledge of the entire manufacturing process and the ability to make decisions on their own. It just naturally makes sense to use teams in such an environment.

The implications of these changes are striking. The best-conceived engineering technology depends on employees who give the job their

Results of Technology

Smart Managing Some key changes resulting from new manufacturing technologies:

- Closer interdependence among activities
- Different skill requirements: usually higher average skill levels
- More immediate and costly consequences of any malfunction
- Output more sensitive to variations in human skills, knowledge, and attitudes and to mental effort rather than physical effort
- More dynamism, that is, continual change and development
- Higher capital investment per employee and fewer employees responsible for a particular product, part, or process

Consequences of AMTs	Work Team Contributions
1. Interdependent activities	Work teams become skilled in interacting, sharing jobs, confronting problems, and team effort.
2. New skill demands	Cross-training, shared responsibility, use of statistical and other problem-solving tools characterize team training.
3. Smaller margin of error	Work teams are typically responsible for the quality and quantity of their work by reducing errors and decreasing variability.
4. Greater dependence on people	Work teams have the capacity to learn, flex, and develop new sets of operating guidelines as the work demands change.
5. Output dependent on judgment, commitment, and attitude	The level of drive, internal motivation, and commitment among workers will make vast differences in productivity and quality.
6. Large capital investment	With their high level skills, ability to conduct on-line maintenance, changeovers, and adaptations, work teams can get the most out of sophisticated new equipment, specialized processes, and costly new materials.

Table 3-1. Advanced manufacturing technologies and work teams

total commitment and concern for quality. Smart managers can greatly promote success by teaming their employees, allowing them to combine their knowledge and skills to be more responsible for a greater part of the work process.

As is evident from Table 3-1, the new skill sets demanded by the new machines and processes of advanced manufacturing technologies require judgment, initiative, creativity, and an orientation toward improvement. Not only do teams work well with the new technologies, they thrive on them, providing the flexibility and expertise to cope with the new demands.

Is the Work Appropriate for Teams?

We began this chapter with the big question: How can you determine if teams are right for your business? We've discussed various driving forces and restraining forces and several major trends transforming the ways we do business. That's all been to provide you with general issues to consider.

Now we focus our question more, to guide you in thinking more specifically: Is the work appropriate for teams? Which activities and work areas in your organization would benefit most from teams and would most favor that approach?

You probably wouldn't start your teams program with a group of lawyers who are working on separate cases, accountants in a financial accounting department responsible for various specific auditing functions, or research scientists working in their own labs. Why? Because the work they do is not integrated. Each can probably operate most successfully alone without help and support from the others.

Employees who work alone, are responsible for a process or a job, and would benefit little from regular interaction with others in similar jobs are unlikely to fit into the team model. In fact, they often reject the notion in the strongest terms, preferring to be left alone so they can do their work. When their work is reorganized—if we were to group the accountants around business units rather than by specialty—then teams would make sense.

Four Criteria

Here are four criteria to help you decide whether or not to develop teams for a specific process or activity. Your jobs should meet at least two of the criteria. If they don't, think twice about initiating teams for that process or activity. Your employees may not see the point, or they may run into so many problems that the attempt won't be worth the trouble.

1. **Judgment.** Does the work call for complex decision making? Are workers expected to make judgment calls on significant aspects of planning, execution, or improvement?
2. **Complexity.** Is the work technically sophisticated? Are workers expected to master many intricate details, learn them well, and be able to perform without significant additional instruction or supervision?

3. **Shared Responsibility.** Is the successful execution of the work contingent on more than one process? Do workers need help from others in order to do their jobs?
4. **Labor-Intensive.** Does the work depend on labor rather than on analysis or mechanical processes? Do outputs, in terms of both quality and quantity, depend on the actions of people rather than on machines?

Are Your People Ready for Teams?

OK. You've thought about your business needs, about driving forces and restraining forces. You've considered work design and organization. You've started assessing processes and activities to decide which would benefit from teams. So, you're about ready to start teaming. Right?

Wrong! This is about *people*. You face one more question, perhaps the most important: Are your employees, supervisors, and managers ready?

The best gauge of readiness is whether people in your organization are *acting* ready. Are your employees cooperating and collaborating in their usual interactions? Are your managers committed to getting input before they make decisions? Are your supervisors acting more like facilitators than nannies or cops? Have you experimented with teams, perhaps for projects or as a task force? How well have they worked in your particular environment?

> ### To Team or Not to Team
> **Smart Managing**
>
> That's not (necessarily) the question.
>
> We've been discussing the use of teams as if it were a case of "either ... or"—employees work either individually or as teams. But in some situations it would make more sense to team employees for certain activities, but not to form a work team.
>
> That may be true for your sales reps, for example. They might continue to work their territories individually, but team up to strategize for new opportunities or to work on solving problems they all face. Are they a team? Well, yes ... and no.

Those are the basic questions. Other factors to consider include:

- past experiences with participatory management
- the extent and nature of management and supervisory training
- labor relations
- support from corporate headquarters
- financial stability of your organization
- job stability
- overall interest of employees in working in teams

When you analyze these factors, you're likely to come up with a few more issues to consider. These questions have no simple answers. We can't offer you an instrument to help you make your decision. (Sorry!) All we can do is challenge you to examine your situation from every perspective and to be honest and realistic about what your efforts reveal.

So, What Do You Want?

Smart Managing

Pick a job, any job. What do you expect from your employees?

- Do you expect them to use their judgment?
- Do you expect technical sophistication?
- Do you expect them to share responsibility for work tasks?
- Do you expect their efforts to matter, for employees to be more than just hands to hold tools and operate machines?

If that's what you expect from your employees, congratulations! You've identified processes and activities that teams could do well.

A Question More Important than Answers

At this point, you might be feeling like the only answer to the big question—"How can we determine if teams are right for our business?"—is "We can't!" Well, you're right. But how often in business do you find "a sure thing"?

The point of asking this big question and all the others that it generates isn't to come up with an answer. It's to better understand the advantages and disadvantages of teams for your organization, to help you explore the opportunities, and to examine the potential problems. In fact, the more thought you invest in asking and answering questions now, the less effort you'll need to expend later to help your teams succeed.

Let's summarize the main points of this chapter:

- **Evaluate your business reasons for using teams.** Don't get involved in teams just because "it's a good idea." That's not a strong enough driver to sustain the effort required for teams. Competition, technology, quality initiatives, downsizing, or reorganizing may provide good business reasons for starting teams.
- **Make sure the work is organized in ways that can benefit from a team effort.** If you have a shop full of individual contributors, you'll need to redesign the work to fit the team concept ... or abandon the idea.
- **Assess your current climate and culture.** Do you act like a successful team organization now? Do your employees have a team spirit? Do your managers and supervisors both talk and walk the team philosophy? Are your employees and their unions interested? You may already be "doing teams," so you're ready to move ahead in a more organized and planned manner.

You may decide that teams are right for your business. But your business may not be right for teams. Again, using teams is definitely not like using a new machine. You can't decide that it makes sense and then just start. You've got to make sure you're ready for teams!

The following guidelines should help you.

- **Move very slowly at first,** do the planning up front, and don't make any changes in the workplace until everyone understands what you're doing. When creating teams, or introducing participatory decision making of any sort, it's

> **CAUTION!**
>
> **Slow: Teams Ahead**
>
> Move slowly with teams. Plan your objectives, goals, structures, needs, and potential problems. Make sure the people involved know, understand, and support what you're doing—before you make any changes.

tempting to move quickly. Confusion and vague goals and objectives are often the results.

- **Understand the strengths and weaknesses** of your organization. Anticipate problems and plan ways to prevent them or at least to minimize the effects.
- **Get the support of stakeholders,** particularly unions if they play a role, before introducing any change that might seem threatening to anyone in your organization.
- **Include all the stakeholders** when administering any survey and assessing survey results: senior management, operational managers, administrative management, MIS, accounting, and human resources. They may have the power and determination to address deficiencies at once and help your organization be more ready for teams.

Teams can be great for your organization—but only if you're ready for them!

Here's the bottom line. If your organization is not ready, *don't introduce teams.* If you try, you're almost certainly going to fail or, at best, to create a situation that's difficult and painful for both managers and employees. It's just not worth it.

Manager's Checklist for Chapter 3

- ❑ Treat teams like a business initiative. Link the success of your organization to the success of the team initiative, so your teams get the support and involvement they need.

- ❑ Don't think of teams just as a *concept.* Evaluate their potential in terms of your specific business and your particular organization, in terms of what you need to do and how and in terms of driving and restraining forces.

- ❑ Focus on the big question: Are teams right for your organization? Get specific: Is the work appropriate for teams? Which activities and work areas would benefit most from teams and would best fit that approach?

- ❑ Make sure your employees and managers are ready for teams. How are they doing their work and interrelating now? What are the prevalent attitudes and feelings?

Why Organizations Have Problems with Teams

Scenario:	Four Clients and a Consultant
Scene:	A seminar on self-managing teams
Players:	Client from Public Sector
	Client from Manufacturing
	Client from Service
	Client from Healthcare
	Consultant (the seminar leader)

Public Sector: This empowerment stuff is great, but there are just too many decisions that need to be made by management. If we let the teams really have responsibility for decision making, we could get into trouble.

Manufacturing: Our team empowerment program worked well at first, but then the teams wanted to do too much. They wanted to get involved in decisions they weren't ready for.

Consultant: How did you know they weren't ready?

Manufacturing: They messed up, and we had to go in and change their decision.

Service: Empowering our teams has been a qualified success, but we had to pull back on our empowerment goals.

Consultant: What do you mean by your "empowerment goals"?

Service: You know, letting the teams do their own hiring, budgeting, planning, and day-to-day scheduling. The teams started meeting all the time, and their work suffered. The first thing they suggested was to reorganize the office.

Consultant: I can see how that could be tricky.

Healthcare: Our team program started out great. We gave our program unit teams all the empowerment they wanted.

Consultant: What do you mean by "all the empowerment they wanted"?

Healthcare: Well, we let them do everything: make their own schedules, hire new people, work with the suppliers, and deal with patient relations and insurance companies. You know—everything.

Consultant: Everything. All at once?

Healthcare: Sure! Isn't that what empowerment is?

Consultant: Before I answer that, let me give you all some feedback.

If you recognize yourself or your organization in the concerns of the clients in this scenario, you're not alone. For every success with empowered teams, there are maybe five failures or at least highly qualified successes.

Scary, huh? But if you can anticipate the problems, you can act to prevent them or at least minimize their damage. No matter how optimistic you may be, you can benefit from the heavy dose of realism in this chapter.

Five Major Potholes

Problems in empowering teams range from the mundane and predictable—"Management didn't really want teams and didn't support them"—to the more subtle—"Our work structure tends to reward individual effort rather than team accomplishment." I've identified five major potholes that many organizations fall into when trying to create self-managing teams. I'll first describe these potholes, then provide some general guidance for avoiding them. Finally, I'll offer some tips on guiding and supporting teams through their five stages of development and filling the potholes typically encountered in each stage.

Pothole 1: The Dump

The most common pothole along the road to empowerment is "the dump." The dump occurs when management decides to try the team concept, holds a short meeting to work out the details, decides that the process is basically a "no-brainer," and then delegates to teams 27 key duties that were formally the province of management.

The result—open rebellion—astonishes the managers. But why are they so surprised? After all, how would the managers react if their bosses decided to triple their duties?

The problems associated with the dump arise from several flawed assumptions. Let's look at four of them.

Balance Optimism with Realism

The best way to avoid mistakes in developing teams is to balance optimism with realism. You've got to believe in teamwork, of course, but you've also got to understand human psychology. You've got to trust that your teams will eventually succeed, but you've also got to realize that it won't happen quickly or maybe even very naturally.

From the start of your team initiative, maximize on the power of teamwork. Don't involve only managers who are staunch proponents of teams or who are generally idealistic. Balance your managerial team with some people who tend to ask a lot of questions, who find problems, who are maybe even suspicious of teams. You'll have a more balanced perspective— and demonstrate the benefits of diversity for teams.

Assumption #1: Everyone wants to manage and be in charge. Managers tend to assume that employees are interested in authority, because that's what interests the managers.

Fact: Many employees are skeptical about managerial roles. They see managers coming in early, leaving late, and trapped in interminable meetings. Somehow they're not motivated by this scene.

Assumption #2: The assignments that are delegated to the team members are simple and easy to pick up—handling their own time cards, staffing the shift, scheduling routine maintenance, planning the vacation schedule, and so forth.

Fact: When the formal power of the supervisory position is removed, even the simplest jobs, such as monitoring the use of safety glasses, may be complex. The problem isn't in the task, but rather in the social issues of who's in charge, how employees give orders to their peers, how team members deal with conflict, and how teams handle personnel problems.

Assumption #3: When workers can take responsibility for the *whole* job, they'll be able to produce higher-quality products and services.

Fact: Most workers *already* feel they're doing a quality job.

⚠ CAUTION! ⚠

Test It Out!

When you've worked out the rough details of your team initiative, run the plan past a few of your employees before you unleash it.

It's easy to do a focus group. Ask employees to volunteer one or two hours of their time. You might hold the meeting during lunch and provide the meal. Make sure your volunteers represent a good cross-section of the employee groups that the team initiative would affect. (Some managers may need to exercise their persuasive skills to fill out the focus group.)

Choose somebody to facilitate the discussion and somebody to take notes. The second job is easy: enlist a secretary. But who'd make the best facilitator? Somebody who can ask neutral questions, probe without intimidating, clarify confusion, and answer questions. Then, keep the managers away and bring in your focus group. After the meeting, be sure to thank them—they may have saved your organization from a minor disaster!

Adding more work, including self-managing work, *interferes* with the job they're doing. So, in their minds, greater responsibility means lower, not higher quality.

Assumption #4: Team members are people with homes, mortgages, kids to raise, lawns to mow, and taxes to pay. They can easily learn to handle work activities similar to the tasks they do in their private lives, like budgets, staffing, housekeeping, and resource planning.

Fact: First of all, not everyone gets those tasks done on time and with the degree of quality demanded in a business environment. Second, there are systems, procedures, people, and forms that complicate those activities. Learning new tasks and adopting new behaviors requires both technical and interpersonal training. Employees should begin with simpler tasks, then advance to the more complex. Handing a team a lot of jobs at once will only cause havoc.

Now you understand the four major assumptions that lead to the dump—and you know the facts so you can deal with them.

Pothole 2: The Bait-and-Switch

A second pothole that can endanger your team initiatives is "the bait-and-switch." That's when the managers offer more than they're willing to give up. Whether the move is intentional or not, the effects can ruin your team effort.

The bait-and-switch works like this. The managers hold a meeting in which they explain the vision and values they've laboriously developed with the help of the consultant. Since they're very proud of their vision, they expect the team members to get excited too. Moved by a zealous fervor, they may say a few things they later regret.

Here's an excerpt from a talk given by a very enlightened plant manager in a start-up committed to self-managing work teams. His quotes are followed by some typical interpretations of his message by employees.

He said: "We want to have the highest-quality product in the industry produced at the lowest cost."

They thought: Good! That means they'll have extra money left over to give us raises and bonuses.

He said: "We want everyone to share their ideas and participate in the decision-making process."

They thought: It's about time. I'm going to tell management
exactly what I think about the way this place is organized.

He said: "We expect teams to take the initiative in planning
and organizing their own work with little direct supervision."

They thought: Great! We don't have to listen to our supervisor.
We can do our own thing.

He said: "We want teams to hold their own meetings and solve
production and quality problems on their own, working
directly with customers and suppliers to achieve the high-
est levels of quality possible."

They thought: Good! We'll keep meetings off-limits to managers and supervisors. We can bypass purchasing and
accounting and cut our own deals with suppliers.

Because of this kind of misunderstanding, managers, who
may mean well but communicate imprecisely, are cast as the
villains when teams start blasting away in all directions. While
it's great to have a vision, you must get specific when you
communicate that vision. There may be nothing worse than a
vision that's shared ... but understood differently.

As we'll show later, the best way to ensure successful
empowerment is through a sliding scale of structured
responsibility "handoffs." Managers must develop a detailed
implementation plan that follows their vision but carefully
defines and regulates what teams do, how, and when along
their journey toward self-management.

Pothole 3: Read My Mind

Very often managers want teams, but don't know what they
want the teams to do. They may have done some easy reading
on empowerment and, since they want to downsize anyway,
see teams as the natural vehicle. Or they expect teams to
relieve them of the less interesting managerial responsibilities.
They fall in love with the potential, but their objectives are
vague and they have no strategy for achieving them. Why not?
Because they're confused about *how* to empower.

> ### Danger! Words at Work
> **CAUTION!**
>
> When you communicate anything abstract, it's always a good idea to provide a simultaneous translation into practical terms. Abstract expressions tend to send our minds in different directions, depending on our experiences and expectations, our hopes and fears.
>
> To avoid this natural danger, attach your high-flying thoughts to some down-to-earth actions. After we use such abstractions as "participate in the decision-making process" and "take the initiative," we might translate, "This means you'll attend meetings and provide input, but not have final say," for example, or "We'll ask you to offer suggestions, but not make any decisions."

So, what happens? With the best intentions, but very limited understanding, they announce their plan for teams, provide some team-like training, and then just hope the idea works.

But it usually goes quickly out of control. The results aren't quite what the managers expected. Disappointing? Yes! Frustrating? Of course! Surprising? Not at all ....

The problem is there from the start. Let's sit in on the company meeting in which management enthusiastically announces its plans for empowerment. The president chooses her words carefully, but to the employees those words are frequently punctuated with "read my mind."

Here's what the president says about the empowerment process—with the mental reactions of the future team members in parenthesis:

Thank you all for joining us today (We had to come!) in this, our first empowerment meeting. (What's empowerment?) We're embarking on a new method of management (What's wrong with the old one?) and seek your input on how to improve our quality and service. (So that's why they fired the old boss!)

From now on, we want you to take a more active role in helping to manage our business (Somebody's getting promoted!) while continuing your excellent work as members of teams. (Uh-oh! No promotions, just more work.) We expect teams to begin to take on more responsibility (What does that mean?) and have a say in day-to-day decisions that

> ### Describing the Future
>
> **TOOLS**   When your managers meet to discuss a team initiative, get specific about the future. Try the following:
>
> Ask each manager to take five minutes or so to write down a description of how his or her unit will be functioning with teams one year from now. What will the teams be doing? How? What will the manager be doing? How? How will the teams connect and coordinate with teams in other units?
>
> Then, have each manager read his or her description to the others. After all the scenarios have been presented, the group should discuss any differences of perspective, using the discussion to help refine their expectations for the team initiative.

impact the running of the business. (What decisions?) We want our supervisors to take on a whole new role (Who's going to cover for us when we're sick, then?) and team members to take on many traditional supervisory duties. (You mean we'll have to fire ourselves?)

In the meantime, management will work collaboratively with teams by becoming more visible and accessible. (Oh no, they'll be on our backs all the time now!) We look forward to working hand in hand with team members (You mean the managers will be out there getting dirty and sweaty with us?) and asking for team participation in management meetings. (Does that mean we'll be invited on the golf outings from now on?) In the future, we hope to run a leaner, flatter organization (Layoffs—I told you!) where quality is first (Does that mean we can stop reworking all those junk components we get?) and we demonstrate respect for all people. (Finally, they'll get rid of the time clock!)

Too often, that's the end of the "read my mind" message—and the start of the pothole. Management may provide the employees with a little training toward working as teams: how to communicate, run meetings, solve problems, deal with conflicts, and so forth. But when it comes to actual concrete tasks and assignments, either the managers move right ahead to the dump, or they equivocate with the bait-and-switch.

This read-my-mind pothole may, in part, be an unintended result of visioning exercises that give managers the idea that visioning is a cerebral, poetic activity that teeters on a delicate balance beam between imagination and action. While it's true that visioning requires a short detour through the right hemisphere, a vision can only be communicated through words and actions. (Much more on this in Chapter 5.)

A vision without a clearly articulated action plan is a hallucination. Managers who try to share their vision without also defining an action plan are likely to go from "read my mind" to "read my lips" when teams start going off in their own directions—which they'll do sooner or later without a plan.

Pothole 4: Yes, but ...

The fourth pothole that endangers team initiatives is the dreaded "Yes, but ...." You're probably familiar with this one.

Sometimes management, with the best of intentions, delegates a set of duties to the team, but then has second thoughts about that decision. Sometimes that pothole opens up when the team makes a mistake, but it also often develops overnight when a manager suffers from a "What if ...?" nightmare. That speculation generates a concern. In other words, the "What if ...?" becomes a "Yes, but ...."

Three problems that management hasn't anticipated or, at least, hasn't resolved generally are the underlying causes of the "Yes, but ..." pothole.

Problem #1: Lack of home office or corporate support. The team idea starts locally, in a branch office or one of the plants, without approval and support from the very top. So, local management acts timidly, feeling guilty and afraid of getting caught. They hesitate to empower the teams because they don't feel empowered themselves.

Problem #2: Lack of supervisory support. Sometimes top managers interpret "participation" as something that happens between them and the employees. They go down and visit "the trenches." They attend meetings and team presentations. Unfortunately, they may neglect to involve middle managers and supervisors. Conflicts develop. The neglected middle managers and supervisors find fault with the teams. The top managers, penitent and skittish, withdraw from the process and perhaps even lose interest and lessen their support.

Imagine Why Teams Wouldn't Work

Do you want to avoid mistakes? Use your darkest imagination.

Take the plan for your team initiative and let your fear run wild. What worst-case scenarios can you imagine?

Managers stress the art of problem solving, but they tend to neglect the art of problem *finding*. Try to shoot holes in your team plan. Try to find loose ends that might cause your project to unravel. Push it through the most punishing torture test you can devise.

Then, of course, apply those problem-*solving* skills!

Problem #3: Over-identification with the team's success. This is the "shadow syndrome," when interest becomes an obstacle and support becomes a burden. I've seen plant managers get so involved with the teams that they become overprotective, fearful that the least misstep foreshadows a colossal failure. As a result, the team members never learn by doing, they rely on the managers, and they learn to avoid responsibility.

The solutions to problems 1 and 2 are pretty straightforward: Get support from *all* stakeholders before embarking on the team journey.

Handling the third problem takes a little more sustained effort. You may have good reasons to fear that the team will make catastrophic mistakes, but you can reduce that possibility by providing initial supervision. Allow small mistakes on small tasks. The team will learn the value of anticipating potential problems and breaking down big projects into smaller actions. They also will learn invaluable emotional lessons that can only come from failure.

Pothole 5: Try It—You'll Like It!

This fifth pothole is a variation on the old theme, "Do as I say, not as I do." The image here is of managers reassuring teams that the water is fine without having set foot in it themselves. The employees know what's happening, and so do the managers. The result: The employees are reluctant to take a plunge into team waters, and they trust the managers less.

This pothole also may develop from a lack of planning. The managers know that teams are a good idea, but they themselves don't really want to spend the time and effort it takes to become a team.

This situation is not uncommon. In fact, in my experience, managers are seldom willing to go through the same paces as they require of the team. They rarely attend training programs in team skills. Their meetings last too long, they're poorly planned, and they usually result in more meetings. Managers fail to empower each other. They deal with conflict obliquely, if at all. They avoid quality tools and techniques.

What's the natural result of this "Do as I say, not as I do" attitude? Yep! The employees learn from the actions, not from the words. They assume that teams are impractical, difficult, and dangerous—because otherwise they'd make as much sense for managers as for employees.

The situation may not be quite that simple, of course. Sometimes managers, while providing an environment suitable for teams, can't benefit from such an environment themselves. They may be constrained by higher management structures and expectations, demands from the outside, and political power plays.

Maybe that situation sounds familiar. If you find yourself in that position, unable to practice the teamwork that you preach, here are some tips to help your employees appreciate your bind and know that you're sincere in promoting teams.

Tip #1: Tell them the truth! Remarkable, but simple advice. Explain what's keeping you from being a team player. In my experience, teams will understand your situation and the problems you face.

Tip #2: Go slow. Delegate and empower at a cautious pace. When you delegate too much too quickly, you're more likely to find yourself having to change course or risk being perceived as wavering in your support.

Tip #3: Pick one commitment action and stick to it. A commitment action is an activity that shows you're practicing what you preach. If using quality tools is critical, use them in management meetings. If safety is a top priority, never go on

You're the Role Model!

Smart Managing   Many managers regret that they're unable to form teams, to practice the teamwork that they preach, because of organizational constraints. But that really shouldn't worry them—not as much as the reality of their situation.

The reality is that they're already serving as a model. When managers meet for hours, yet accomplish little or nothing, that's a model for their employees. When managers play political games or repress differences into passive-aggressive behaviors, that's a model for their employees.

What kind of models are you and your fellow managers?

the shop floor without full protective gear. If you're promoting good interactive skills, avoid acting like Attila the Hun, even when production is slipping or people are arriving late.

In summary, there are many shortcuts to empowering teams, but most of them have potholes. Self-managing teams will thrive and grow, but only when managers plan appropriately, involve all the stakeholders, and change the organizational culture.

Filling the Potholes

A little later in this chapter you'll find a series of tips on guiding and supporting teams through their five stages of development and filling the most common potholes in each stage. But first, some guidance of a more general nature.

Despite all the experience we can tap, the lessons learned from successes and failures, developing self-managing teams is not wholly a science. It's also an art, when we try to fit a process to a unique location, special business needs, personalities, and a history.

In implementing teams, stay loose, avoid blame, roll with the punches, take things one day at a time, and apply almost every other cliché in the book. That's because expertise adds very little value beyond good old common sense.

But sometimes there's nothing so uncommon as common sense. At the risk of taxing your patience, these few suggestions for the early stages of team development will keep you

Just Let Them Do It!

One of the managers in the company was consider-ably more successful with his teams than his fellow managers. His success was all the more surprising because he had very little managerial experience.

One evening, the secret of his success came out after a col-league ran into him at a local park, coaching a soccer team of six-year-olds—who were playing surprisingly well together.

The next morning, she cornered him by the water cooler and forced out the story of his success. He told how he'd explained the rules of the game, trained the kids in the basics, and then just let them learn by playing—sometimes very badly.

"The essence of working with any team," he concluded, "is to explain the rules, prepare them in the essential skills, and then let them go, coaching from the sidelines as needed."

from hitting the potholes, bottoming out, and getting out of alignment on your road to teams. (If you feel like you know it all and are ready to move on to the next section of this chap-ter, I'd advise you to read these next few pages anyway—just so you're aware of what other readers need to know.)

1. **Have clear business reasons for teams.** I've never worked with a client who didn't have a rigorous business plan. But I've never worked with a client who had much more than a few ideas written down about the team plan. Teams require just as much planning and goal-setting as a plant start-up—even more, in some cases.

   Recommendation: Put together a business plan for teams. Specify why you want teams, what you expect them to contribute, and what goals or milestones you plan to use to evaluate their success.

2. **Get the resources before you get the vision.** There's nothing worse than starting on the journey to teams and running out of power in the early stages. Lots of articles and books say that teams will save money, improve qual-ity and productivity, and help eliminate layers of manage-ment, but most of the literature fails to mention the enor-mous *cost* of a teams program. Most of this cost is front-

end, so don't expect any benefits right away. But you can expect hefty costs in training, overtime, staff or administrative time, higher staffing to accommodate both production and team activities, and necessary team facilities such as meeting rooms, flip charts, and so forth.

Recommendation: Budget 15% of your operating budget for team activities. Assume that for each 40 hours of labor, four to six hours will be spent in team training, meetings, action planning, and related self-development. This is a conservative estimate. If you don't have the stomach or pocketbook for this, don't get involved in teams.

3. **Don't assume that everyone has "religion."** Belief in real participatory management is a little like the gift of faith: You either have it or you don't have it. It's also easy to fake. The single greatest cause of failed teams is sabotage by managers and supervisors who don't really believe in teams and are afraid to go along with what seems a crazy, impractical philosophy.

   Recommendation: No visioning session or teambuilding will change a long-held set of values and beliefs about the role of management. Instead, spend time with managers to clearly define their new roles in the team process. Put these roles in writing and throw out the old job descriptions and performance appraisal forms. Write some that really reflect what managers are supposed to do, such as coaching, supporting, helping with resources and problem solving, facilitating, and praising.

4. **Tell the teams what you expect them to do.** And while you're at it, tell yourself, too. When managers don't give teams a road map for taking on responsibilities, the teams frequently become overly ambitious and get into trouble, prompting management to snatch back responsibilities and authority. A fuzzy empowerment timetable causes much grief among teams and managers, since unclear expectations produce unclear results.

   Recommendation: Try using a "boundary diagram." That's a bull's-eye with each of the circles indicating a period of three to six months. Negotiate exactly which activities you expect from the team during the first few months and write them in the center of the bull's-eye. In the next circle, which represents the second or third quarter, add some more activities. Continue this process until you have several concentric circles that add up to a year or more and encompass a wide range of new responsibilities. The team can use this diagram to gradually acquire more self-management responsibilities in a planned way. It's equally important to identify activities outside the team's boundaries. If you don't want the teams getting involved in sales and marketing, finance, personnel matters, materials ordering, or work station redesign, say so and mark them outside the bull's-eye entirely.

The Team Development Checklist

Now, as promised, here's a simplified checklist of five phases of team development:

I.   The Learning Phase
II. Developing a Strategy
III. Active Experimentation
IV. Testing and Evaluating
V.   Sharing and Growing

Use this checklist as a benchmark for your team programs. For each stage, I've noted some positive actions that have proven beneficial for development, as well as potholes that have consistently caused problems in the five phases (tables on pages 58-62). I've tried to inject a little humor, but these potholes are uncomfortably close to the steps actually taken in organizations that haven't properly prepared for teams.

A Team Development Strategy

Every organization must plan its own strategy to roll out teams. But here's a good example of one organization's strategic plan. Naturally, each step is, in itself, a project or series of projects, as I'll show a little later.

I. The Learning Phase

Potholes	Positive Actions
• Skip learning phase. Declare that you've achieved work teams unilaterally. • Use complex, conceptual socio-technical design language and assume everyone understands "inputs," "outputs," "boundaries," "variances," and other technical terms. • Don't involve upper management or union. Rather, delegate to HRD or lower-level management. • Make no special provisions for budget, training, planning, time, time off the job, consulting, and so on. • Skip vision and values. Simply target only limited short-term business reasons. • Decide right off that this is a simple process, a "no-brainer." • Concentrate on driving forces only, not barriers to change. • Have a norm to do it "our way." Don't listen to what anyone else has to say. • Hire a consultant to facilitate initial planning meetings, then don't require senior managers to attend. • Hire a consultant, then ignore any advice if it goes against your timetable for implementation.	• Establish operational reasons for work teams: e.g., interdependent operations, need for teamwork, new technology, work redesign, etc. • Develop a vision, values, and supporting mission. • Create a project plan, time line, and goals. • Define terms: Work Teams, Facilitators, Team Leaders, etc. • Identify checkpoints and indicators. • Visit other teams currently in operation. • Confront policy decisions, particularly those impacting pay and work rules. • Identify barriers: e.g., contract provisions or corporate guidelines that may place boundaries on development. • Ensure that specific support is available: e.g., money, time, other resources. • Identify a consultant/facilitator who can help provide outside perspective.

1. Create a work plan to achieve our mandate to make our business a team-based success.

    1.1 Gain consensus with key corporate staff on our overall intention to develop a high-performance, team-based organization.

    1.2 Select and hire a consultant who can take us from selection to the development and training of team members.

II. Developing a Strategy

Potholes	Positive Actions
• Avoid the planning stage, stay loose, make the same mistakes over and over again. • Do teams only. Change nothing else. • Hide your failures and boast about your successes. • Research your results for years. • As soon as they become skilled, change the players. • Have a model, but don't write it down or get corporate commitment for it, so it can't be mistaken for "real" policies.	• Establish roles of members, leaders, facilitators, supervisors, and managers. • Identify team boundaries. • Identify other resources and their roles. • Establish phased training. • Establish decision-making and appeals process. • Evaluate links to other structures and processes, including pay, policies, and performance appraisal. • Communicate and publish plan, then check for understanding and agreement. • Gain commitment from stakeholders. • Integrate quality assurance and other sources of data collection and measurement into the process.

    1.3 Hold a preliminary strategy session with the consultant to establish goals and objectives and build a work plan.

    1.4 Plan and get agreement to an ongoing development process.

  2. Develop an overall vision/mission that provides direction to our efforts.

Consensus General agreement or accord. That's simple enough: We all use that term. But do we really understand what it means?

The word "consensus" comes from a Latin word, *consentire*, which comes from two words that mean "together" and "to feel." So, a consensus isn't just about reaching a decision. It's also about how we feel about that decision, about feeling together. And that's a feeling you can't achieve through maneuvering and pressuring.

III. Active Experimentation

Potholes	Positive Actions
• Implement on grand scale. • Print hundreds of brochures so you can't change anything. • Spring it on the union. • Threaten the employees with closings or other disasters if they don't cooperate. • Don't waste time on training. • Do training after everyone complains about not getting trained. • Avoid goals or objectives and evaluate only cost savings and productivity increases. • Meet yearly, if at all. • Get rid of those who can't get with the program.	• Communicate plan to all employees. • Listen and respond to questions and concerns. • Identify and recruit team members and team leaders. • Involve work groups from targeted areas in initial meetings. • Involve internal customers in the implementation. • Develop and deploy team training curriculum. • Develop and deploy manager-supervisor training. • Make needed changes in work areas and equipment. • Agree upon and implement performance measures. • Meet regularly to discuss problems and concerns. • Develop a problem-resolution process. • Deal creatively and empathetically with resistance to change. • Provide individualized coaching and remedial training.

2.1 Hold a vision/mission development session to brainstorm ideas and gather input from the management staff.

2.2 Refine the vision and identify basic beliefs.

2.3 Identify policies that support the vision and beliefs.

2.4 Define the policies and set short-term goals for each of them.

2.5 Communicate our vision, basic beliefs, and policies to employees for feedback and input.

3. Train and develop the management staff.

3.1 Identify training that will help develop and model the behaviors needed to drive the work elements.

3.2 Set individual and team goals for implementing the work elements.

IV. Testing and Evaluating

Potholes	Positive Actions

• Don't measure process variables, since they're too difficult to assess.
• Don't use the scientific method. Just measure everything constantly and add measurements together.
• When you have a good working model, leave it alone. Don't change anything or allow anyone else to.
• Measure only "businesslike" variables like cost and productivity.
• Bring in outside people to do all process measurement and improvement. Don't trust the teams.
• Reward only management.
• Don't get involved in bonuses or profit-sharing; employees might begin to expect it.
	• Deploy for predetermined length of time.
	• Establish new teams.
	• Test and measure variables during:
	  ▪ normal business cycles: slack periods, rush times, change-overs, new technology introductions, downsizing, new product introductions, etc.
	  ▪ the team development cycle turnover in the team
	  ▪ turnover among management
	  ▪ changing market conditions
	• Constantly strive for improvement in all measured parameters.
	• Train teams to do self-evaluation in both process and bottom-line metrics.
	• Reward process improvement, such as team cohesiveness, as well as bottom-line metrics, like productivity and cost.
	• Allow the process to settle down. Don't react hastily in out-of-control situations.

Brainstorm A method of shared problem solving in which all members of a group spontaneously contribute ideas. We use the term a lot, but often incorrectly. In fact, some people apply it to an activity that's basically the old "let's run it up the flagpole and see who salutes it ... or shoots it down."

The original use of the word "brainstorm" is to characterize a sudden and violent disturbance in the brain. Such a disturbance can produce unexpected ideas—some clever, some crazy. But no idea is crazier than limiting your "brainstorming" to a mental version of skeet-shooting. Open it up—and tap your group synergy!

V. Sharing and Growing

Potholes	Positive Actions
• Put together a slick presentation that sells but doesn't communicate your experience. Present it everywhere. • Keep your secrets: consider successful work teams a competitive weapon and guard it closely, so you promote secrecy in your organization and don't learn from others. • As soon as you feel sure of success, stop measuring things. • Make the teams an exclusive club. Keep other employees envious, cynical, and guessing. • If you have a union, immediately try to decertify. • When your team implementation process is up and running, hand it off to HR or some other maintenance organization. • After training the core group of members and managers, stop training. Let new people learn on the job.	• Attend conferences and share your results with others. • Share your results with your corporate office and other divisions. • Involve team members in all team-related activities that involve travel outside the plant location. • Get your customers and vendors involved, too. Have them deal directly with team members. • Expand your program. Adopt a total employee involvement approach. • Continue to encourage teams to take risks and try new things. • Broaden the team's boundaries. • Encourage change and active experimentation. • Begin teams in other areas, such as office, technical, and professional ranks. • Find ways for employees not on teams to have participatory experiences.

3.3 Set performance goals for individual managers and for the team as a whole.

3.4 Develop an ongoing plan to work together to complete our goals.

3.5 Create an ongoing system of management rotation, training, and outside education to help us maintain a world-class team.

4. Identify and train teams.

4.1 Conduct an overall technical analysis to determine the location, size, and placement of teams as our employee base grows.

4.2 Provide basic team orientation that defines our goals and provides team members with an understanding of our vision, basic beliefs, and work elements.

4.3 Define the roles of team leaders, members, facilitators, and so forth. Jointly set goals for the teams and help them create a development plan.

4.4 Provide just-in-time training for the teams. Make sure teams have the skills and maturity to take on new assignments.

5. Identify team boundaries.

5.1 Develop team mission statements that delineate technical systems.

5.2 Teams identify customers and their requirements.

5.3 In conjunction with customers and suppliers, teams set goals and measurement systems to ensure quality outputs.

5.4 Teams set a schedule of task progression that allows them to move to greater levels of empowered decision making in their day-to-day activities.

5.5 Teams and management negotiate performance measures and rewards based on team productivity and business activity.

6. Initiate project activity.

6.1 Work directly with teams on improvement projects focusing first on achieving Quality, Safety, and Productivity and the goals set out in the work elements.

6.2 Train teams in Quality Improvement tools and techniques.

6.3 Provide teams with assistance in measuring their output and in determining the costs and benefits of their project suggestions.

6.4 Identify a reward system to reinforce team activities and team suggestions.

Breaking Down the Strategy Steps

As I mentioned earlier, each of the steps in the team development strategy is actually a project or series of projects. As an example, here's how one of the strategy bullets (1.3) can be developed into a set of action items.

1.3 Hold a preliminary strategy session with the consultant to establish goals and objectives and build a work plan.
   1.3.1   Identify milestones for the next quarter.
   1.3.2   Clarify hiring process and implement the use of the team-screening tool.
   1.3.3   Complete a preliminary plan for team development.
   1.3.4   Identify measurements and goals.
   1.3.5   Create an employee communication and awareness plan.
   1.3.6   Develop a budget for team efforts, consisting of both time and other expenses.
   1.3.7   Identify members of the steering committee, and set dates for additional planning sessions.
1.3.1   Identify milestones for the next quarter.
   1. What are the key issues we see in this project?
   2. What concerns or problems do we foresee?
   3. What are our general, overall goals and aspirations for the next year?
   4. What could go wrong and how can we plan to deal with it?
   5. What are the training and planning targets?
   6. How many days (meetings) can we devote to this project this year?
1.3.2   Clarify hiring process and implement the use of the team-screening tool.
   1. What is our hiring plan to full staffing?
   2. Is the screening tool being used? Problems or other findings.
   3. What statements or basic communications are we using regarding teams?
   4. Do we wish to develop a basic orientation plan regarding teamwork?
   5. Do we wish to use a video or other tool to orient new hires to teamwork?
   6. What communications have we had with management regarding teamwork?
1.3.3 Complete a preliminary plan for team development.

1. Empowerment goals.
2. Roles of leaders and others.
3. Numbers of teams, and numbers in teams.
4. Time available for meetings—when and where.
5. Performance management—teams and individuals.
6. Other critical training—job skills, safety, etc.

1.3.4 Identify measurements and goals.
   1. What are some key indicators of effectiveness?
   2. How can they be communicated, tracked, etc.?
   3. What to do right away? Suggestion system?
   4. Individual development plans?

1.3.5 Create an employee communication and awareness plan.
   1. Awareness: What is a team, your roles, etc.
   2. Implementation plan.
   3. Expectations and responsibilities.
   4. Measurement.
   5. Training plan—what and when. Pre-employment training?
   6. Team structure and timing.
   7. Team leadership.

1.3.6 Develop a budget for team efforts, consisting of both time and other expenses.
   1. Needs: meetings, supplies and other support, locations, tracking, etc.
   2. Meetings: when, where, how often, how long, what (agenda).
   3. Safety and other specific training.
   4. Compute all costs, including time off job, materials, management support time, etc. Have available for review.
   5. Ask area managers to do "down time" analysis and determine best times for team meetings and put together matrix.

1.3.7 Identify members of the steering committee and set dates for additional planning sessions.
   1. Steering committee roles and responsibilities.

2. Normal membership guidelines.
3. Frequency of meetings.
4. Communication strategy.
5. Percent of job time in team-related activities.

Putting together a good, detailed team development strategy is a lot of work. But think about what's going to be involved in your team's initiative—the people, the time, the material resources, the energy, the emotions.... It's a huge investment. There's also a huge payoff—but only if you plan properly.

Manager's Checklist for Chapter 4

❑ If you're trying self-managed teams, know that the odds are against you. For every success, there are maybe five failures or at least highly qualified successes. But you can improve your odds by anticipating the major problems.

❑ Don't assume that everyone wants to manage and be in charge, that management tasks are simple to pick up, that as employees take greater responsibility they'll produce higher-quality products and services, or that team members can easily learn to handle work activities similar to the tasks they do in their private lives.

❑ Be specific when you talk about your teams and what you expect.

❑ Don't panic if your teams don't go perfectly from the start. Don't worry about making mistakes; just worry about not learning from them.

❑ Show how teams work: Managers should serve as models of cooperation, collaboration, and spirit.

❑ Keep in mind that there are five phases of team development, each requiring certain actions and each threatened by certain problems.

Vision, Values, Mission, and Strategy

Ioriginally titled this chapter "Pointing Things in the Right Direction: Creating and Communicating Vision, Values, Mission, and Strategy." Unfortunately, that title was a little long. But I really wanted to emphasize the importance of this phase in team development and give it the prominence it deserves.

Chapter 4 ended with a reminder to form a strategy for team development. The first of the five phases of team development outlined in Chapter 4, The Learning Phase, begins when you create a vision, values, and a mission. That forms a foundation for the second phase, Developing a Strategy.

Any work group—organization, division, or team—needs a vision, values, a mission, and a strategy to give it direction and to move it along. The way those four essentials are created provides a base for success, but the way they're communicated to others allows the group to build on that base. This is particularly true for teams.

I've never worked with an organization that didn't have some sort of theme statement, whether the people called it a vision, a mission, a statement of purpose, or whatever. Yet few organizations have figured out how to make their words come alive and take on meaning beyond the board room or management conference. Failure to do so may not hurt a company measurably, but it can cripple a team. A self-directing or self-managing team without a vision, values, a mission, and a strategy is likely to be inefficient and ineffective. Those four essentials form the core that points your team in the right direction and drives it forward.

In this chapter, we'll discuss visions, values, missions and strategy, explaining how they can guide a team from conception into action and then through to success. We'll focus on teams, but we must stress that the organization must have a vision, values, a mission, and a strategy, and that this core must support teams, teamwork, and empowerment.

Begin with a Vision ... and Values

A team vision expresses a sense of purpose for the team and an idea about what it is expected to achieve. Because the team functions within the context of the organization, its vision should be framed in relation to that larger vision.

A vision can convey central values, like Quality, Customer Satisfaction, Excellence, Participation, Achievement, Being First, Teamwork, Safety, and Empowerment. Values can drive an organization, guiding and supporting its operations and initiatives. As important as it is to express values in the vision for an organization, it is generally even more important for a team. The team functions within the organization and its vision and values; it holds and promotes certain of those values in a special way, perhaps with values not specifically expressed in the organization's vision.

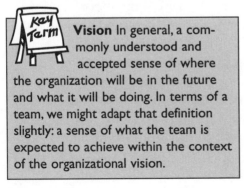

Vision In general, a commonly understood and accepted sense of where the organization will be in the future and what it will be doing. In terms of a team, we might adapt that definition slightly: a sense of what the team is expected to achieve within the context of the organizational vision.

Let's take an example. XYZ Inc. accepts and champions as its core values Quality, Customer Satisfaction, Excellence, Participation, Achievement, Being First, Teamwork, Safety, and Empowerment. XYZ forms a Quality Team and a Customer Satisfaction Team. When they shape their vision statements, the former team might go with Quality (of course!), Excellence, and Empowerment, then add Continuous Improvement, while the latter team might choose Customer

> **Values** Abstractions considered to have real worth and importance. Unfortunately, the connection between *abstract* and *real* is tenuous for many organizations. What happens usually communicates a second definition of values: the pragmatic basic instincts that drive what people do.

Satisfaction (naturally!), Teamwork, Safety, and Empowerment, then add Communication.

In embracing values, it's better to think big. The values behind great visions don't tend to be the rational values of analysis or tradition or even the vague values of participation or customer satisfaction. They're more likely speculative values like achievement, imagination, creativity, and excitement. They're seldom managerial values that control and measure, but leadership values that inspire, empower, and focus.

In developing a team, you're generally going to be more limited in your vision and values than if you were working on the vision and values for an entire organization. You already have a designated purpose, more or less. But it can be deadly if you just take that purpose and try to shape it into a vision, to basically dress up a work assignment in fancy words. A vision should not only guide, but also excite and compel.

Creating Your Own Vision

OK, so how does a team come up with a vision? Who's involved in the process? And how do you recognize a vision?

Three key questions. You'll find the answers in your organization, in the people, purposes, and power behind your team development. This chapter can only guide you.

Who Creates the Vision?

The key players will be the members of the team, of course—if empowerment is to be real from the start. Managers involved in developing the team or who will be working with the team should probably take part in this process, to a greater or lesser extent. The process of creating a vision depends on community, collaboration, and consensus as well as creativity. The best vision in the world is less effective if it's imposed on a team, rather than generated by the members of that team.

What Makes a Vision?

Warren Bennis and Burt Nanus, in their book, *Leaders: The Strategies for Taking Charge*, note that "a vision may be as vague as a dream or as precise as a goal or mission statement." They characterize a vision as "a target that beckons." That's good: It's something we aim at because we feel compelled to.

Does a vision have to be realistic and credible? No, not if it's truly visionary. Should you be able to explain it clearly and concisely? Not necessarily. Should it make sense to you? Yes, definitely! How do you know when you have a vision? When it excites you to do something, when it gives you pleasure and a sense of satisfaction, and when it fulfills your most important values.

Excitement. Pleasure. Sense of satisfaction. Most important values. These are the basics of a good vision. But how do we generate those basics?

Visioning Takes Work

John Kotter, in *The Leadership Factor*, describes visioning: "Too often, I fear, we fall into the romantic trap of believing that great vision comes from magic or divine grace. In the business world, it rarely (if ever) does. Great vision emerges when a powerful mind working long and hard on massive amounts of information is able to see (or recognize in suggestions from others) interesting patterns and new possibilities."

How Do You Create a Vision?

A manager of training and development once tried making a vision happen by sending out copies of Alvin Toffler's *Third Wave,* Kenneth Blanchard's *The One-Minute Manager,* and Tom Peters and Robert Waterman's *In Search of Excellence.* To trigger some significant emotional event, he included Richard Bach's *Illusions*. The senior executives probably appreciated the books, but nothing much came of the manager's efforts. Sometimes wishing and hoping for inspiration just won't work.

Three more direct approaches may yield more tangible successes in a training program situation:
- the intuitive approach
- the analytic approach
- the benchmarking approach

The Intuitive Approach. This method focuses on forming visions through guided imagery and imagination. For the intuitive supervisor or manager, this is less tricky than you might suppose. Many already have what they might call "philosophies" or "management styles." These are essentially ideas and feelings about decision making and leadership. But sometimes these philosophies or styles are similar to a vision—personal, value-based, energizing, and inspiring.

To begin the intuitive approach, ask the participants to imagine the team making an important difference in the organization, fulfilling its purpose(s) to perfection, totally free of the inhibiting constraints of reality. (This simple exercise tends to free imaginations from mundane concerns better than any motivational talk or abstract generalizations.)

Then ask the participants to list all the things they'd like the team to achieve. Push them to list at least 10 items. This will be difficult for some people, because they'll tend to think in terms of constraints.

Next, ask the participants to each prioritize the items on their lists, in terms of importance, not with respect to practicality, timelines, or other criteria.

Finally, ask the participants, one by one, to name the top item on their lists. (If the participants differ in company rank, call first on those at lower levels, so they're less likely to be influenced by their higher-level peers.) After each round, get the group to look for general themes and values expressed in the pool of items. These should provide you with the substance of a great vision statement.

The Analytic Approach. This method of creating a vision builds on the reality of the team's purpose(s) and function, to establish expectations and then aspirations.

A good way to structure this approach is by asking questions, using the "5 Ws and 1 H"—who, what, when, where, why, and how. The order can vary according to your particular situation, the origins of the team initiative, the extent of empowerment, and the context in which the team will function.

You might try the following questions:

- Whom do we serve?
- What do we do?
- When do we do it?
- Where do we want to go with our efforts?
- Why are we focusing on this work and these goals?
- How do we put the above into operation?

It might be more appropriate to answer the "What?" before the "Whom?" and the "Where?" before the "When?" You might want to move "Why?" up on your list, maybe even to use it as your initial question. In general, it's best to put the "How?" last, for two reasons—because it tends to limit the freedom and scope of the discussion and because it leads naturally into the next step, the mission statement.

The Benchmarking Approach. The intuitive and the analytic approaches frame the vision process within the context of the organization. Benchmarking, on the other hand, looks outside the organization for ideas and inspiration from competitors.

The visioning process driven by benchmarking is practical and drives the participants to investigate how other organizations are using teams and how those teams are working.

To use the benchmarking approach, follow these steps:

- **Choose your models.** Ask "What teams are successfully doing what our team is expected to do?" (You might not find all the benchmark teams in organizations in your particular field. There might be great quality teams or customer service teams, for example, in quite different organizations.)
- **Examine the visions of those teams.** Ask "What ambitions and values are guiding and driving these teams?"

- **Build on those visions.** Ask "How can we do even better?"
- **Test your vision.** Ask "How does it feel to succeed in our quest?" If your answers are positive, if you feel fulfilled, then you've probably got a great vision.

The Six Cs of Visioning

OK, now. You've used one of the three approaches—intuitive, analytic, or benchmarking—or some combination. So, let's imagine that you've got what you consider a great vision. (If it doesn't feel *great*, but merely *good* or *solid* or *appropriate*, it's probably not really a vision.) Now what? Well, let's test it.

A vision statement should be simple and clear. It might involve personal growth, business success, and/or the role of people, customers, and/or products. Regardless of its content, it should have certain characteristics that make it work for the people who need to be guided by it. Here is a set of principles that govern good vision statements. Use them in brainstorming your team's vision. The vision must be:

- **Clear**, easily understandable.
- **Concise**, short and specific.
- **Connected**, related to things people do regularly.
- **Compelling**, conveying a sense of urgency.
- **Contrasting**, different—and better—than what we do now.
- **Credible**, something we can do, that's worth doing, and that everyone supports.

Creating a great vision is tough. But once you've got it, you know you've really accomplished something. You'll be proud of your vision—and use it to lead your team.

Most organizations seem to have their visions everywhere in sight—on the walls, on the stationery, and on awards—but nowhere inside, not in the hearts and the minds of the people. A vision is too often a set of lovely words that have little real effect. That's bad for an organization, but it can be fatal for a team. In developing a team, you've got to create a vision with soul and then shape it so it's also got muscles.

Missions Mean Muscles

A vision keeps you focused above and beyond the horizon, while a mission statement keeps your feet on the ground,

Key Term

Mission Statement
A practical elaboration of your vision, a sort of job description for the team. It should set forth purposes, responsibilities, authority, methods, and resources, as well as any specific areas of responsibility and authority for individual team members.

moving you toward your goals. A mission statement defines the team's job, what it's expected to do.

As with the vision, what you develop as your mission statement and how you develop it depend on your situation. The mission statement establishes your empowerment, your presence and purpose, your values. Think of it as your job description. It outlines how you're going to pursue your vision and promote your values.

Your mission statement should establish such essentials as purposes, responsibilities, authority, methods, and resources. If members have specific, individual areas of responsibility and authority, these should be defined as well. You might also want to append a list of the members and any "expiration date."

Strategy: Planning for Success

Now that you've got your vision and your mission statement, what do you do? You put them to work, immediately!

At this point you need a strategy. You need to turn your mission statement into an action plan. The word "strategy" comes from two words in ancient Greek—*stratos*, "army," and *agein*, "to lead." In simple terms, your team is an army, your vision and values are your reasons

Key Term

Strategy A plan that sets down specific ways and identifies specific resources with which to overcome specific difficulties to achieve specific objectives.

for going to war, your mission statement is to win that war, and your strategy is what leads you to victory.

Your strategy is basically an elaboration of your mission statement, broken into specific actions, to attain specific objectives, within specific time limits.

When you created your vision and embraced your values, you were *idealistic*. When you established your mission statement, you were *positive*. Now it's time to get *realistic*. In this phase you consider the difficulties, the problems, the barriers, and the obstacles—and how you plan to face those difficulties, solve those problems, knock down those barriers, and overcome those obstacles.

How? Well, again, that depends on your mission statement. But the following can provide guidance as you meet to plan your strategy and then as you put it into action:

- Determine how to measure your progress.
- Identify the difficulties.
- Set your goals.
- Decide on your tactics and actions.
- Build support for your efforts.
- Put your plans to work.
- Evaluate the situation continuously.
- Focus on your successes.
- Reward achievement.

Determine How to Measure Your Progress

You outlined your team objectives in your mission statement, explicitly and implicitly. Now, how can you measure your success in terms of each of those objectives?

Now you need to put such ideals as "improvement" and "satisfaction" and "collaboration" into terms of quantitative assessment. How will you know if you're improving a situation? How will you know if you're increasing satisfaction? How will you know if you're promoting collaboration?

Identify the Difficulties

OK. This one should be easier. What's keeping you from achieving each of your team objectives? Physical limitations? Time constraints? Budgets? Prevailing attitudes? Company policies? Work procedures? The personalities of several key people? Traditions?

Be specific. The more specific you can get, the better your chances of overcoming those difficulties.

There are two guidelines to keep in mind as you discuss the difficulties challenging your team:

- **Keep pushing.** There's rarely just a single difficulty. Identify a difficulty, then ask, "What else?" Repeat until you've identified a few for each objective—or you're exhausted.
- **Keep probing.** Things are rarely as simple as they seem at first. Examine a difficulty, then ask, "Why?" You'll better understand the difficulties you face—and generate some ideas about how to overcome them.

Set Your Goals

You have ways to measure your progress toward your objectives, and you know what difficulties lie in your path. Now you match them up and set realistic, specific goals.

When should you expect results? In three months? Set a goal for that point. Then set another for six months, another for nine months, and so on. Keep two factors in mind: the force of momentum and the law of diminishing returns.

Decide on Your Tactics and Actions

When you identified the difficulties to overcome, you also discussed causes, reasons, and other matters involved. Now, you do a little problem solving.

For each of the difficulties identified, come up with at least one or two approaches. Then, for each of those approaches,

---

CAUTION!

Choose Your Metaphors Carefully

Beware of the power of metaphors.

It's natural to express things metaphorically. In particular, many managers talk about business in terms of sports or military operations. Such comparisons can be positive, powerful ways to help employees understand and feel more motivated.

But we tend to forget that the power of metaphors can also have a negative influence. Some employees may not care about sports, for example, or be familiar with the terminology.

Know your employees. Plug into their interests. Talk in terms of their experiences. Be creative. Make metaphors work for every member of your team.

list specific actions and decide who will be responsible for each of those actions—individuals, pairs, or small groups.

This may take a lot of time and thought. But it will be worth it when you can focus your efforts effectively and use your resources (particularly time and energy) efficiently.

Build Support for Your Efforts

Your team is not alone—at least not necessarily. You've got a vision that should inspire your fellow employees. You've got a mission statement that promises results for the organization. You've got a strategy that shows you mean business.

Part of your planning should be to identify allies and ways to enlist their support. Who can help your team? How can you involve them in your efforts?

You may decide to approach certain people, managers in particular, before you act and to inform them about your plans. Others, such as influential veteran employees, might be more readily convinced by results, so you'll want to plan to approach them after accomplishing something.

Spend some time with your potential allies individually. Let them know what your team is doing, how they can contribute, and what you expect of them. Ask for their support and commitment. Answer their questions and try to solve any problems they might have with what you're doing. Don't compromise your principles, but seek ways to achieve your goals with maximum support and minimum resistance.

Put Your Plans to Work

You're on your own here—but you should have some great action plans! As you put your plans to work, evaluate the situation continuously. Things change—and not always as anticipated. It's wise to meet regularly to discuss any unexpected changes that might impact on your strategy. Be flexible, ready to adapt to changes in your situation.

Evaluate the Situation Continuously

Of course, in your regular team meetings you should evaluate your progress. Review your goals. If you've attained a goal, should you revise your expectations for subsequent goals? If you've fallen short, what should you do differently?

Focus on Your Successes

Regular meetings also provide the opportunity to celebrate your progress and boost the enthusiasm and energy of the team members.

You should find reason to celebrate at every meeting. No need to break your budget on champagne and caviar, but you can surely allow yourselves a few minutes to enjoy the fruits of your labors. Leaders who try to keep their armies ever focused on the battle, without allowing them a chance to celebrate their victories, will find that they're left with bodies going through the motions while the hearts lie on the ground behind.

But don't limit your celebration to team meetings. Show the entire organization what your team is achieving. Your team members will get greater recognition from their peers, and your allies will share in the glory of your success.

Post progress reports on bulletin boards. Make presentations at management meetings. Provide your company newsletter with articles outlining your efforts and the results and (of course) acknowledging the support and commitment of your allies. Be positive about the results of your work, but be honest and don't indulge in hype: Embellishment and exaggeration will only cheapen your achievements.

Reward Achievements

Rewarding achievements is a natural part of focusing on your successes, with a slight challenge. You celebrate your successes as a team, of course. But how do you reward achievements? That can be a big question, whether we're talking about financial compensation or symbolic recognition.

It might be easy, if responsibility for specific actions has been distributed among individual members, pairs, and small groups. But, whatever you decide, you should consider the culture of your workplace. Rewards should inspire the team, improve teamwork, and encourage greater efforts. Otherwise, you allow your success to breed failure.

Lead the Way ... from Within

Conspicuously absent throughout this chapter is the mention of leadership. Why? Because we've focused on team efforts—and because good leaders know how to be part of the team. They recognize that team members are more likely to participate more actively and develop teamwork if the team leader plays a less dominant role in the process. That's how you lead—from within, working among your teammates.

Of course, when there are problems, particularly difficulties with specific work areas and their managers, you may need to use your people skills and (if necessary) your position to help your teammates deal with the problems. But don't intervene too quickly. Show your teammates your confidence in their ability to handle the situation—particularly if it involves conflicts among team members. (In Chapter 10, we'll discuss ways to help team members deal with internal problems.)

So, as the team leader, you're basically just like any other member of the team? Yes, but more so. You can perhaps best show your leadership in the team process by serving as a model, by playing your part as well as you can.

You're also a leader in assuming responsibility for the bottom line, the results achieved by your team. By "responsibility" we don't mean credit, of course. We mean that it's up to you to get results. If the team succeeds, the credit belongs to all the members of the team, including (but not especially) you. If the team fails, it's because of you.

There's a saying that comes to mind here: "Success is a child with many parents, while failure is an orphan." The true leader adopts that orphan.

That's the harsh reality of being a good leader. But if you're committed to the team process and to your teammates, if you work hard as an individual member and as the leader, you can almost guarantee success for your team.

Manager's Checklist for Chapter 5

❑ Every team needs a vision, values, a mission, and a strategy.

❑ Create the team vision by using an approach appropriate to your culture and thinking—intuitive, analytic, benchmarking—or by combining approaches.

❑ A team mission statement establishes empowerment, presence, purpose, values, responsibilities, authority, methods, and resources.

❑ A team strategy elaborates on its mission statement, breaking it down into specific actions to attain specific objectives within specific time limits.

❑ Lead your team from within, as part of the team. Your employees will develop into a team more effectively and efficiently if you play a less dominant role.

Team
Dynamics

The study of team dynamics provides insight into why teams do what they do at different stages of their development. This is important, since knowing in advance what kinds of challenges to expect will help the team deal with them.

Understanding team development is critical for both the leader and the team members. In this chapter we'll review a model and provide tactics that teams can use to handle problems and opportunities at each level.

How Teams Are Supposed to Develop

Teams, like individuals, go through cycles of development, becoming progressively more capable of self-management. Here's a four-phase model that describes the process.

1. **Forming.** The "honeymoon" phase. This period is characterized by excitement, anxiety, and a feeling of power. Teammates must get familiar with each other before taking risks. Not much productive work. Progress may be marked by false starts unless managed carefully.
2. **Storming.** The "post-honeymoon" phase. Here egos clash, personality differences become obvious, opinions

differ, and frustration grows. At this stage, ideas are proposed and challenged, plans are laid and revised, and new directions are put forward and evaluated.

3. **Norming.** The "reality strikes" phase. Norms (standards or accepted codes of conduct) develop gradually through consensus. Members get to know and understand each other. Productivity is good, but not outstanding. True strengths and weaknesses become clear and the team begins to form a routine.

4. **Performing.** The "synergy" phase. The team develops and grows. It's a learning machine that can adapt to new situations with minimal difficulty. It's truly a business unit, rather than a work team. Relationships are clear and a consensus has been established about the team's direction. Goals are oriented toward tasks, rather than relationships. The group can achieve significant results.

How Teams Really Develop

OK, that's the typical developmental process for teams. But what really happens is more like what's depicted in Figure 6-1.

Each of the four phases may be marked by problems. Table 6-1 (on page 84) shows the warning signs and recommended actions for the leader to take.

How to Identify, Diagnose, and Treat Common Team Problems

An overheard conversation between an Operations Manager and the Director of Human Resources at a mid-sized company:

Operations Manager: Why did I ever let you talk me into teams? They're nothing but trouble. I have to spend all my time in training and meetings, and we're behind on our production schedule.

HR Manager: Well, you were the one who wanted to try teams, remember? We went to visit that car company, and you fell in love with their program.

Operations Manager: I know, but obviously something is wrong

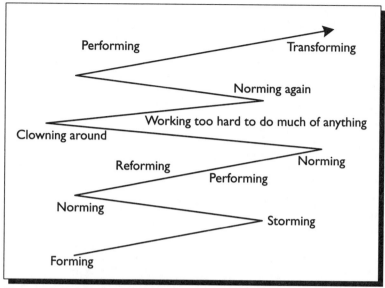

Figure 6-1. How teams really develop

here. Maybe they were giving us a song and dance there.

HR Manager: I don't know. Maybe we ought to look at ourselves. What are we doing that's causing the problem?

Operations Manager: Why is it always us? Management is
always to blame. We don't spend enough money, we don't
spend enough time, we're not committed enough, we lack
vision. Maybe it's not *us.* Maybe it's *them!*

Maybe it is and maybe it isn't. A lot has been written about
the failure of managers to develop successful teamwork. Lack
of a long-term vision, insufficient commitment of time and
money, inadequate planning, skimpy training, and too little
coaching are causes of team failure that arise when managers
want results but aren't willing to make sacrifices to get them.

But what about the teams themselves? Sure, managers
need to get serious. But team members need to take responsibility for their own problems and shortcomings, too.

To learn more, we asked some team facilitators about what
they considered typical problems with teams regardless of
management commitment and support. We also asked them

Warning Signs	Leader Actions
Forming Stage • Silence, little communication • Questioning purpose of team • Low trust or commitment • Challenging the leader • Unfocused brainstorming • Disagreement as to problem • Too much talking and wandering • No one takes responsibility for action • Seeks simple solutions (money, staff) • Underestimating problem difficulty	**Forming Stage** • Select members one by one • Explain purpose of team • Present clear problem statement • Set goals, timetables, etc. • Maintain sense of urgency • Agree on ground rules for meetings such as duration, behaviors, etc. • Coach problem members outside the meeting • Follow up on assignments • Get members' bosses involved
Storming Stage • Cliques begin to form • Unrealistic expectations arise • Members develop at different levels • Realization of problem difficulty • Desire to delegate problem upwards • Unwilling to challenge or confront	**Storming Stage** • Encourage differing points of view • Keep focused on time and goals • Break down large problems • Seek small successes • Coach members individually • Allow conflict to surface
Norming Stage • Arguments occur for no reason • Anger is directed toward team leader and management • Team sees the world as "Us and Them" • Talk is a substitute for action • Subgroups go in their own direction • Unanticipated problems break down momentum	**Norming Stage** • Challenge the group to conduct analysis to resolve disagreement • Move from directive or coaching to supportive leadership style • Share leadership duties • Insist members share responsibilities • Use tools and techniques religiously • Stick to your goals and time tables
Performing Stage • Team takes on too much • Members resist leadership • Members operate autonomously • Team communication breaks down • Members resist boring work • Team runs out of motivating problems	**Performing Stage** • Allow the team to set its own course • Enforce regular meeting schedule • Make frequent presentations • Get involved in larger projects • Move toward self-managing teams

Table 6-1. Team development tactics

for solutions. All the facilitators agreed that there are no guaranteed solutions, only best guesses and good ideas.

So, here are the problems they reported and their suggestions, which I've classified into 10 categories.

When Do We Join the Board of Directors?
(Coping with Unrealistic Expectations)

Hiring, training, and creating employee teams is a big deal for most organizations, but it's an even bigger deal for the individual employee who, in most cases, hasn't had this much attention from his or her employer. Team members sometimes feel a heightened sense of importance and status.

While this kind of commitment is desirable, it can lead to unrealistic expectations and then to frustration. Team members may sulk, decide that they've been misled by management, and begin to focus on the things they *aren't permitted* to do, like set their own production quotas, rather than those things they're *encouraged* to do, like begin work on time without monitoring. Teams may spend their meetings inventing new products rather than planning safety audits. Facilitators constantly have to remind them to focus on their work.

We advise teams to confine their initial problem solving to their "circle of influence." That sphere surrounds their immediate inputs and outputs, as shown in Figure 6-2. When the team starts meddling in things too far up or down the line, the members get too far from their base and their input becomes less useful, since they know less about the process.

Recommendations

- Don't oversell the team concept. To recruit the best, use the team concept as a lure, but don't present unrealistic visions. Make sure people understand the job first.
- Show the team a time line. If you have plans for self-direction, lay out a plan that shows how you're going to get there. Team members must understand that they can't rise magically from apprentices to bosses.
- Identify boundaries right away. It's just as important to specify which activities are not within the province of the

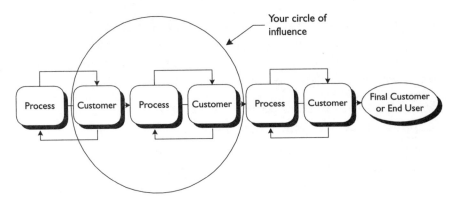

Figure 6-2. Circle of influence

team as it is to specify the activities that are. Be perfectly clear about the limits of team decision making. Restate it as frequently as necessary.

- Explain the importance of what the team is doing right now. The job is first just a job, not a role or a process. The most critical criterion for team success is the ability to do a quality job.

Whom Can We Fire? (Wanting to Do Too Much Too Soon)

One of the best ways to charge up a team is to present a picture of a successful self-managing work group. When new team members see videotapes of very advanced teams doing budgeting, business planning, and, most dramatically, hiring and firing team members, they sometimes get carried away with their own potential.

It's great to be enthusiastic, of course, but a

> **⚠ CAUTION!**
> ### Circle Pains
> As teams develop, members are likely to feel more and more frustrated with the limitations of their circles of influence. Managers should then find ways to expand those circles, at least by opening lines of communication throughout the organization, if not also by forming cross-functional teams.

lot of tickets have to be punched before any team is ready to participate in a delicate personnel activity like hiring or firing fellow employees. Part of the problem is that hiring and firing is so traditionally the *manager's* role that the appeal of that kind of power is likely to render the most fair-minded team member faint.

Words like "hiring," "promoting," "paying," "firing," "disciplining," and "coaching" are highly charged. Talking about them too soon can make all the other jobs—time reporting, cross-training, safety responsibility, phone coverage, vacation scheduling, and so forth—pale in comparison.

Recommendations

- Avoid talk of hiring and firing unless you intend to train the team in those areas within a few months. Such talk can distract from day-to-day activities.
- If you plan to train the team in selection or discipline, make sure the team members understand that "input" doesn't mean absolute discretion in personnel decisions. We have *never* run into a team that makes *final* hiring or firing decisions. Even the most progressive team organizations limit the team's input to making recommendations.
- Develop and communicate clearly the role of the supervisor or manager. Make sure everyone knows that managers, not teams, make critical personnel decisions.

The Tortoise and the Hare (Differences in Work Styles)

While slow and steady may win some races, it loses others. In teams, members with the work style of the tortoise must learn to work side by side with the speedy hares. Work styles affect pace, detail orientation, job skills, flexibility, and safety.

How we work reflects both our personality and the way we've been trained. Were we taught to maintain a fast pace, dealing with errors later on? Or were we rewarded for getting it right the first time, even when it meant going slower? Did we work in an organization in which safety and quality were #1 goals? Or were production and volume emphasized?

Conflicts about work style surface more quickly in teams than among individuals working independently. When output depends on each team member taking responsibility for a share of the work, work styles impact productivity, which can influence how the team is rewarded.

Most teams have room for different work styles, but you must set minimum requirements to avoid conflict. Pace and quality are standards that all team members must maintain equally, while job rotations can often allow for different kinds of work. Sometimes the range of jobs allows for different work styles, but dumping the less demanding jobs on the slower or less skilled workers can create resentment within the team.

Recommendations
- Maintain standards. There's only one solution to the issue of different work styles: maintain the same standards for everyone. Equality fosters mutual respect in teams.
- Balance all jobs. If a team rotates through several jobs, don't make some really hard or others really easy, so team members don't dread them or crave them.
- Encourage respect for different styles through training. Make sure team members understand that it's OK to solve problems or approach challenges or conflict differently, while maintaining a consistently high work standard.

No Time for Talk (Focusing on Results but Ignoring Process)

Unlike the Japanese approach to quality improvement, which stresses following a carefully defined problem-solving process, organizations in this country often spend too much time emphasizing results while failing to provide training in the processes to yield those results over the long term.

The idea that the team can be tougher on itself than any first-line supervisor has been validated time after time in many industries. Without a supervisor to balance their work, teams that are paid partly on the basis of their results will push themselves to the limit. They'll skip meetings, avoid training, fail to do preventive maintenance, violate safety procedures—in short, behave just as if they had a straw boss over them, cracking the whip. Money, fear, and competition can drive the team harder than the most traditional overseer.

If this situation continues, conflict arises within the team and teammates blame each other. Pretty soon the team breaks down into a number of workers out for themselves. Benign neglect can cause teams to do their own training and personal development, planning, strategizing, and dealing with change and conflict, while learning the ropes of team dynamics on the go. Unfortunately, when production calls, personal growth takes a back seat.

Recommendations

- Budget enough time to allow teams to hold regular weekly meetings and follow-up sessions. This is often far more time than management assumes. Altogether, time for meetings and project work, training, and general communication briefings may consume as much as 10% to 15% of overall work time during the first few months.
- If it's impossible to spend four to six hours weekly in training and meetings, go slower, but target the key process skills you want to build. These may include meeting skills, conflict resolution, and basic problem solving. Select process skills that can be used frequently on the job. And use on-the-job time, which is often loosely recorded anyway as training time.
- Go even slower. Don't try to get anything done in meetings, for now. Basic communication is nearly always the most critical need. Spend some meeting time—maybe just a few minutes—talking about work, working together, and solving small differences. Let it go at that.

Throwing in the Towel (Quitting at the First Obstacle)

Many teams are so hyped on their new power and responsibility that they aren't aware of an impediment that often can kill their initiative—the first unanticipated obstacle. Obstacles are many and varied, old and new. You've heard the litany of why you can't do things. It goes like this:

We've never done it that way here.
Where are you going to get the funding for that?
We don't use that kind of equipment.
We tried it once and it didn't work.

*Mr./Ms. So-and-So will never let you do that in his/her
    department.*
*Just wait for a while: your problem will be resolved by the
    upcoming reorganization.*
*Collect some data on that before you implement, say about
    two years' worth.*

Unanticipated obstacles also come in the form of real barriers that may be too complicated or long-term to yield to a new team's ideas.

But whatever the nature of the obstacle, the teams get discouraged. They may think that it's their fault or the system is stacked against them. Rather than accepting that no change is effortless, they may just give up on further risky efforts.

Recommendations
- Plan for failure. By considering resistance and possible failure, team members can develop a contingency plan. They don't stop at that brick wall; they just reroute.
- Avoid large-scale projects as first efforts. The consequences of failure are greater, and management will want a full accounting that the team may find intrusive.
- Work several projects at once. Some will inevitably succeed, while others run into problems. Use them as learning experiences.
- Train team members in potential problem analysis. Show that there's actually a science for anticipating problems.

It's Management's Fault (Blaming Managers for Everything)

Management takes a lot of criticism about not having the long-term vision and consistent values to support teamwork. Some of it's deserved, but some isn't. Many managers get discouraged when their hard work, the time they spend with the team, their efforts at listening and interacting, and their new leadership skills and participatory styles go unrewarded. If they're self-conscious and introspective, they might wonder, "What am I doing wrong?" If not, they may just give up in disgust, blaming the team, the philosophy, the times, or the type of people they hired. Neither reaction is productive.

When team members blame management for everything, it expresses a dynamic of team powerlessness. Most causes of this problem involve a lack of trust between team members and managers. The reasons for this lack of trust include the following:

- The team members never really accepted changes imposed upon them. They went through the motions of becoming a team but didn't internalize team values.
- The managers don't share important business information with the team, so the team attributes all changes that impact it as arbitrary.
- The managers are making arbitrary changes that they should either avoid or leave to the team. Nothing can demoralize a team more than a front office move seen as disruptive and arbitrary.
- The managers are not seen walking the walk and talking the talk about teamwork.
- The team includes one or more persuasive management-haters whose strong feelings can sway the others. We'll talk more about this later.

Recommendations
- Build trust through personal interactions. Attend meetings, walk around, and spend time with the team.
- Maintain a strong, fair, individual appraisal system. Keep in touch with individuals and strengthen a personal relationship. Take active responsibility for coaching and for praising.
- Keep the team current on business information, changes taking place, and shifts in the business climate that may affect management actions.
- Fully empower the team to make decisions that impact only the team.

It's Not My Job (Resistance to Changing Work Roles)

Symptoms of the resistance to changing work roles include the familiar complaint, "It's not my job," along with other, more subtle expressions like:

I've never done that before.
I haven't been trained in that.
That's management's job.
Do I get a pay increase for doing that?
Why me? I did that job last month.
Get one of the new people to do that.

Many problems in teams, including those arising from job rotations and the lack of advancement opportunities, fall into the category of resistance to change.

Most of us seek stable, predictable work. Traditional jobs that could be explained in a half-page position description and mastered in a half-day training program are becoming scarce. Instead, team members are asked to learn several jobs, be ready to switch jobs, move into leadership positions, master new skills, and still work at a much faster pace than they did a few years ago. It's little wonder these kinds of changes, when not accompanied by equitable rewards, are resisted.

Because start-up businesses can hire people both willing and interested in variety, they experience the "It's not my job" phenomenon less often than organizations introducing the team concept to a traditional workforce. Resistance occurs most often in unionized workplaces where job duties took years to negotiate. But wherever job duties and titles were cherished, resistance to change is strong and understandable.

Nowhere is this resistance stronger than among supervisors and managers. Many have not only had their job duties changed, but have also been asked to change the ways they communicate, give instructions, and use their power. Position power has given way to personal power—and they're not just different kinds of power, they're complete opposites.

No one is exempt from the pain as our workplaces change. Businesses must change to stay competitive. It's not a matter of how to remain the same, but of how to introduce changes, how to deal with those who are negatively affected by the changes, and how to reward those who make the transition.

Recommendations
- Make sure that what you're asking for is reasonable.

Break the changes up into small parts and introduce them
gradually.
- Be sure that *everyone* is seen as being asked to change.
There shouldn't be any exemptions.
- Treat those negatively affected by change with respect
and care. Supervisors and other employees who lose their
authority and whose concerns are ignored can poison the
rest of the team with bad attitudes and grievances that
may have some merit.
- Involve the team in strategizing the change. Ask for their
input and work with them on putting the changes in place.
- Make sure there are sound business reasons for change,
and communicate those reasons to the team. It's surprising how much better they understand when they see the
big picture.

One Rotten Apple (Peer Pressure Within the Team)

With all this talk of teams and working together, it seems
unfair to single out any one person as a problem. But for various reasons some people don't belong in teams, and many of
them can negatively affect their teammates. In short, they may
be natural leaders who aren't headed in the direction management wants them to go.

Not everyone who disrupts the team is an undesirable,
however. Some may be good workers who are badly placed or
who haven't found the right match for their talents. Each case
must be judged separately and dealt with in a manner that
seems fair to all concerned. The wholesale termination of team
dissidents will make everyone on the team feel more vulnerable.

Recommendations

Here are several kinds of dissidents and tactics for dealing
with each.

The Genius: She knows a lot of right answers and masters the
job easily. In her search for more, she becomes dissatisfied
and frustrated.
- Use her skills as team leader or for special projects.
- Put her on an accelerated job rotation system.

Silent Sam: He doesn't mind the work and gets along, but he simply can't participate in any kind of team discussion. He's a drag on meetings and too shy to share ideas or get involved in projects.
- Provide assertiveness or similar training.
- Buddy him up with a more assertive co-worker.
- Shape his behavior by giving him progressively more public jobs.

The Steward: He thinks he's working for the union. He feels it's his duty to oppose management on principle. He has a misplaced vision of the labor-management relationship and sees it as a perpetual struggle.
- Let the team as a whole deal with his complaints, real or imagined, on the spot, in detail whenever they arise.
- Deal directly with him on performance issues, including performance during meetings.

The Underemployed: She's working under her intellectual or physical ability or may be overtrained for the job.
- Ask her for suggestions on expanding or otherwise enriching her job.
- If she's qualified, assign her leadership responsibilities.
- Use her as a teacher or coach for other team members who need help.

The Overemployed: He's really not qualified for the job, due to poor skills or lack of training.
- Pair him up with someone who's underemployed.
- Find him work he can do and reposition him in the team.
- Consider terminating him.

Getting Along (How Team Members Communicate with Each Other)

Most teams cite "communications" as the single most critical problem they face. What they mean by this, of course, varies.

In one study, done at a firm that spent thousands of hours and millions of dollars on its teams program, team members said they wanted more information, wanted it faster, and wanted it delivered better. In short, they asked for an improvement in the content of the communications as well as the style.

Follow-up showed that their *content* concerns focused on management. They simply wanted more information on the business and speedier decision making. But their *style* concerns focused on other team members and on other teams. From peers, they wanted more courtesy and understanding.

Working in a high-performance team throws people close together under conditions of stress. The demand for fast-paced and high-quality work creates opportunities for collaboration, but it also lowers the threshold for conflict.

Sources of conflict *within* teams include how team members ask for help, how they deal with problems, and how they handle issues of who's at fault, personal work style, time pressure, work load, and so forth. Sources of conflict *between* teams include customer-supplier relationships, resource availability, work space usage and cleanup, quotas, and rewards.

Yet how members communicate with one another on a daily basis may be the most critical source of conflict in teams. They need to be able to listen, provide feedback, give instructions or convey information, and participate in both one-on-one and group discussions. To reinforce teamwork and defuse conflict, they need to be able to withhold judgment, acknowledge one another's contributions, deal fairly with problems, and display openness. Conflicts can flare up when team members are aggressive, attack each other's ideas or opinions, fail to allow others to express their opinions, avoid group interactions, or try to take over the group.

Though many team members come to the job with good interpersonal skills, it's important to ensure that every member understands the basics of communication and is trained on how to interact in a team environment. You organize teams to improve performance, but they can maintain excellent levels of productivity and quality only through participation and shared problem solving. Successful teams constantly evaluate both their *output* and their *process*—how they're communicating in order to achieve results. Improving communication style is as important to the developing team as improving work methods, and they must take it just as seriously.

Recommendations
- Make sure everyone has good "baseline" skills. These include asking open questions, practicing active listening, and using "direct dealing" to get along with others in conflict situations. (We'll discuss this technique in Chapter 10.)
- Ask, "How are we doing?" by encouraging the team members to periodically assess their "team spirit."
- Create a norm for politeness and respect by discussing good behavior and by seeking and rewarding examples of it.
- Seek peer feedback during reviews. This can be a real eye-opener, both within and across teams. Get teams to force-rank team members according to a number of pre-selected categories, such as output, quality, cooperation, knowledge, and helpfulness. Do the same across teams against appropriate criteria. Use the rankings to allocate discretionary rewards.

Key Term

Force-rank To sort a given number of people or things according to a given order based on given criteria. The process provides *objective* results in situations that are naturally *subjective*. Employees might be divided into categories (e.g., top 10%, next-highest 20%, middle 40%, next 20%, bottom 10%) or prioritized (e.g., first, second, third, ... with no ties).

The Little Engine That Couldn't (Persistent Performance Problems)

No matter how carefully you screen, test, train, coach, measure, or provide incentives, some folks just can't or won't carry their own weight. Our experience with high-performing teams indicates that the rate of poor performers may run between 10% and 15% in the first year or so of the team's life cycle. That's a significant drag on productivity and morale.

Poor performance may result from poor selection or training. But even with the best selection systems and the best training programs, you can still have a few poor performers. Training and selection costs are high, so you want to get the best people and keep them. Turnover of 15% to 30%, while common in many industries where pay and skills are low, is not cost-effective. In a tight labor market, it's very wasteful. It pays to focus on the types and causes of poor performance and to build systems in the selection and training process that deal with them early on.

Performance problems that emerge in work teams are similar to those found in any work environment. They involve competence, motivation, and personal behavior and habits. But because work teams place special burdens and responsibilities on members, some unique consequences for performance arise, including the following:

- Discouragement over the pace of job growth. Team development is generally slower than many team members expect. Teams develop at the pace of the average member, not the star performer.
- The reality of equality. Despite all messages to the contrary, many team members believe that if they work hard and excel, they'll be promoted to a supervisory job. It's tough to fight that belief, especially since most managers hold similar values. Our society encourages individual effort and expects a lot from people with talent. Teams create a cultural conflict, as individuals must work together as peers.
- A perceived imbalance in the workload. It's difficult to divide a complex process so that everyone does equal work. So, some do harder, dirtier, more dangerous and demanding work more often than others. Usually, it's the best workers who get the most work. The adage, "If you want something done, give it to the busiest person," holds for team members as well as for managers.
- Too little job skill training. Modern team jobs often involve a skill set not readily available in the job market. In addition to all the interpersonal skills described in this chapter, team members must have technical skills, including knowledge of computers, maintenance, safety, financial matters, and general business.

Unfortunately, most start-ups and team conversions in existing work groups are under such pressure to deliver results that there's little or no time for training. Many companies push new employees through a 40-hour orientation and training blitz that's intended to cover everything. Not only is the curriculum limited, but the retention rate is low.

Recommendations
- Improve or institute individual performance management. Just because we're working in teams doesn't mean we're no longer individuals with personal aspirations, needs, and goals. Few sources of work motivation are better than a positive boss-subordinate relationship. This can only be attained through personal interaction, feedback, and growth. A good performance appraisal system can foster this relationship or identify poor performers more quickly.
- Maintain and support an active job rotation system. Job rotation systems seem inefficient, unwieldy, and hard to maintain at first. They require a lot of care and provide little short-term payoff. But they're important for overall team satisfaction and performance. They allow for frequent job changes, facilitating cross-training and reducing boredom. They help balance less desirable and more desirable jobs, and they give everybody a shot at leading meetings, teams, and projects.
- Provide more nontraditional training in off-the-job settings. With so little time for classroom training, employers need to be creative in finding good off-the-job training. There are very few training self-study packages available for team skills, but there are good products for technical training. This is an important source of learning, particularly if results are measured by the performance appraisal system. Community colleges also offer training opportunities in evening or weekend courses. An increasingly useful form of training is with audio- and videotape. Professional production of tapes is expensive and time-intensive, but you can put a half-hour welding demonstration, for instance, on a cassette and ask team members to take it home and pop it in the VCR. That may not be too intrusive on their personal time—and may be just as interesting as watching an episode of *This Old House.*

Let's Get Real!

The Lowe's Companies, a home repair superstore chain, are experimenting with teams at their newer distribution centers. To help hire the right kind of people, they've produced a video that covers both the positive and negative aspects of working in a distribution center.

The tape discusses salary and benefits, but also shows the working conditions, which include heavy lifting and extreme temperatures. The idea is to give candidates a balanced picture of the work teams, so new hires will have realistic expectations.

- Provide more realistic job previews to prospective employees. Discuss all aspects of jobs—both positive and negative. Help your employees develop realistic expectations from the very start.

A final bit of advice for both management and teams on how to get along and succeed is simple, yet difficult: "Practice, practice, practice." Good teamwork depends on the basics— job goals, skills training, boss-subordinate communications, performance management, and a focus on both process (daily practice) and results (outstanding performances).

Manager's Checklist for Chapter 6

❑ Know what teams do during the stages of their development and why. That knowledge will help you anticipate problems, challenges, and opportunities so you can help the team deal with them.

❑ A common model of team development consists of four phases: forming, storming, norming, and performing.

❑ Team facilitators have identified problems with unrealistic expectations, overly ambitious aspirations, different work styles, a focus on results while neglecting process, dealing with early obstacles, blaming management, resistance to changing work roles, peer pressure within the team, communication, and persistent performance problems.

New Roles for Leaders of High-Performance Work Groups

Over the last few years, the responsibilities of leaders have changed dramatically. To some extent, the change is a result of participation, the quality improvement movement, downsizing, worker training, and teams. But it's also because the "old" model no longer works very well.

The "old" model of leadership put the leader at the center of the work group. This meant that the leader could control most of the communications between team members. Under certain circumstances, this model worked well, but it was based on several key assumptions. If the assumptions were flawed, the leadership model was less effective.

Assumption #1. The leader alone possessed critical business information. He or she was the sole source for information concerning production, planning, resources, and deadlines.

Assumption #2. Group members had carefully planned jobs and didn't need to communicate with one another.

Assumption #3. The leader had time to serve as the conduit for all necessary communications among group members. He or she was there to listen and transmit information.

Assumption #4. The leader had sole responsibility for the process, so he or she had to control all aspects of it.

Assumption #5. The leader was physically present at all times. As the center of the group, in control of all interaction, he or she had to be there in case any problems arose.

Today, those assumptions are no longer valid. In the new workplace, there are fewer traditional leaders—managers or supervisors. Those leaders who remain don't have the time to micromanage every detail of the work, nor can they be expected to screen communications among team members. Most important, employees have been asked to assume responsibility. With this new responsibility must come a degree of authority. And with authority comes leader-

ship. With everyone acting a little more like a leader, there is little room left for the traditional leader.

The last few years have forced many leaders to make changes in the way they work and communicate with employees. They've had to move from the center of the

> **Old and New Leaders**
> *Smart Managing*
>
> Traditional leaders need to have control over the processes for which they are responsible. New leaders give employees more responsibility and authority over their work. If you consider these approaches, you will see that traditional practices nearly always undermine performance while new leadership practices enhance it.

work group to its periphery. This move means they have to act more like team members whose specialized role adds value to the team.

The Six Roles of a Successful Manager

In the heyday of its quality program, which in 1989 made it the first company in the United States to win the Deming Prize, Florida Power and Light identified six roles that characterized the successful manager in times of change. Those roles were exemplified by managers who thrived during the cultural transformation resulting from the push for the Deming Prize. Though the roles were identified in connection with a quality improvement effort, they fit the model that managers must adopt for a high-performance work group program.

1. **Coordinates Team Activities.** Rather than just supervising, the leader learns to coordinate the team in its activities. That means providing direction, support, and help. It means coaching and exercising influence. It does not mean day-to-day supervision and decision making. (Chapter 9 is devoted to coaching.)
2. **Advises on Problem or Opportunity Selection.** In keeping the team focused on objectives of importance to the overall quality and business plan, the leader plays an active role in guiding the team to select and work on specific priority projects.
3. **Provides Resources.** Without adequate resources, staff members can't do their jobs effectively. Larger organizational goals are hard to keep in focus when the group lacks the means to perform daily operations without stress and frustration. The leader plays a critical role in keeping others in the organization attentive to the needs and capabilities of his or her group.
4. **Coaches on Problem Solving.** The coach's job in problem solving is to learn the problem-solving model, master the tools and techniques, and work directly with the team to maintain momentum and keep it focused on its tasks.
5. **Assists in Implementation.** Helping individuals and teams make things happen is one of the most vital roles of the leader. Many team members need help in understanding the larger organization, making presentations, or working with other departments. The leader can facilitate by working outside his or her functional unit and by gaining support for the team throughout the organization.
6. **Provides Formal and Informal Recognition.** In most organizations, the formal means of recognition are specific, limited, and rarely immediate enough to provide reinforcement. Informal recognition is the best tool to keep staff members motivated between raises and promotions.

Unfortunately, these changes in managerial roles don't come without some resistance. A study by Janice Klein of Harvard University showed that supervisors had mixed feelings about employee involvement programs. While 72% saw them as good for the company and 60% saw them as good for employees, only 31% felt they were good for supervisors.

The same study pointed out that the initial concerns expressed by supervisors had to do with job security, extra workload, and job definition. While their first two concerns are normal and expected, their third, *job definition*, can be considered a danger sign, since one of the most critical factors in a team transition involves getting supervisors and managers to accept and adopt a new role.

The Seven Bases of Power

Leaders inspire their team members to do what they want them to do, either through fear or some other more desirable kind of motivation. These are called the *bases of power.*

Position Power. This power belongs to the leader simply because he or she has the job. "I'm the manager," the leader says, "and you'll do what I say because of that alone." This approach works unless team members are expected to do more than the minimum or to work without direct supervision.

Personal Power. The leader *earns* the respect of team members because he or she spends time listening to them and works to meet their needs while concentrating on organizational objectives.

Expert Power. When serving as a resource, the leader can truly add value by virtue of his or her expertise. The leader can contribute from technical experience, work experience, maturity, or the ability to bring many skills to a problem situation.

Resource Power. The ability to control valued resources is a source of power. A manager is able to control others and exercise a kind of leadership by withholding or providing something in demand.

Reward Power. Like resource power, the ability to confer meaningful rewards is a way to exercise power. When the leader holds the reins on money, promotion, or desirable assignments, he or she can exercise power.

Coercive Power. The ability to force others to act through fear of negative consequences is the most primitive power base, and it can be very effective. The weakness is that, without fear, followers will not be motivated to obey the leader.

Connection Power. This power is based on political and social relationships, on who you know and how well. Power is established through networks. It's passed on from boss to subordinate based on a combination of friendship and performance. This can be a positive power base that all good leaders use—if they're able to fit into the networks and if they make an effort to play positive politics for the benefit of their work unit.

Using Power Effectively

Which of these seven power bases works best with each of the six new roles of leaders? Which others might help you make the most of each role? To be truly effective with teams, you should focus on the fit between your roles and power bases.

A leader has many responsibilities in coordinating team activities, so it may be difficult to keep track of them all or even prioritize them. In the rest of this chapter, I'll review the main areas of responsibilities and their key activities.

Leadership Self-Analysis

Read the following checklists and select activities to use in your own leadership plan. If it seems overwhelming at first, choose certain activities that you should start right away.

Coordinating Team Activities

- Identify teams and team members.
- Coordinate with other managers who have teams on similar projects.
- Coordinate with departments responsible for inputs and outputs.
- Ensure that team activities are coordinated with other work in the unit.
- Ensure that team meetings are taking place.
- Keep abreast of problem-solving activities.
- Be familiar with staffing levels and overtime.
- Keep the team up to date on business issues.
- Attend team meetings to evaluate participation and leadership.

Advising on Problem or Opportunity Selection

- Assigns or helps develop themes or projects.
- Provides information on important business indicators that impact the unit.
- Interacts with the team during initial brainstorming and problem identification.
- Collects and discusses key customer data and input.
- Suggests problems that affect unit or company goals.
- Helps focus problem-solving efforts on achievable goals.
- Advises when problems selected are already being tackled elsewhere.
- Coordinates with other groups when problems are cross-functional or cross-team.
- Indicates problems of which the team may be unaware.
- Communicates quality, productivity, safety, and other expectations clearly.
- Maintains a schedule of team meetings and works with the team on its projects as a peer.

> **⚠ CAUTION!**
>
> **It's a Privilege**
> Working on a team is a responsibility and a privilege. Take care that the members of your team don't see only the responsibility and forget about the privilege they enjoy. And take care that others in the work unit don't regard team members as a favored group.

Providing Resources

- Plans staffing and workload to allow for team meetings and improvement activities.
- Balances workload with team activities and maintains momentum in both areas.
- Budgets for and obtains specific resources, such as meeting locations, meeting times, training, and materials for problem-solving meetings.
- Identifies and provides human resources, such as appropriate internal or external customers, other managers, or technical support.
- Ensures that jobs and shifts are properly staffed to support the workload.
- Works with other leaders to share limited resources.
- Solicits input from the team on future needs and provides for changing demands in workload.

- Discusses with the team the different kinds of resources available to it.
- Trains the team in the budget cycle to ensure a realistic approach to resource acquisition.
- Helps create a team resource list and checks it regularly to ensure that the team's needs are being met.
- Plans ahead to ensure that teams are never left without critical resources when the leader is absent or unavailable.

Coaching on Problem Solving

- Is familiar with the process improvement problem-solving model and the tools that support each step.
- Prepares and asks questions at each step to help the team continuously improve its problem-solving process.
- Seeks expert help in technical problem-solving matters, when necessary.
- Plays an appropriate role at each step in the problem-solving process.
- Helps the team set up guidelines to measure and monitor its problem-solving activities.
- Coordinates additional problem-solving training as needed to bring new members up to speed quickly and to keep abreast of new developments.
- Maintains momentum by creating a sense of urgency about the quality problem-solving process.

Assisting in Implementation

- Ensures that people outside the team are enlisted to support team projects.
- Prepares the team for management presentations.
- Guides the team in avoiding potential pitfalls in working in the larger organization.
- Helps the team implement the improvement and share the improvement and standard operating procedures with other departments.
- Keeps the team on track with time frames, costs, and schedules involved in the new project.
- Coaches the team on the potential problems that often result from changing a process.

- Helps the team gain the support of others for its changes.
- Ensures that new resources—such as training, equipment, time, and money—are available to support a process improvement.

Providing Formal and Informal Recognition

- Helps sponsor recognition events, such as informal parties, celebrations, and appreciation days at the close of important improvement events.
- Works to get his or her team appropriate official recognition for its problem-solving efforts.
- Finds opportunities to praise team members and leaders.
- Lets others know when someone on the team has achieved a significant goal.
- Takes the time to complete and track an individual development plan for each team member.
- Measures the cost/benefit of solved problems and seeks rewards for the team.
- Supports team efforts by regularly reporting problem-solving results to upper management. Being a team leader takes a lot of work. The new leadership model is more complicated in many ways than the old model. As I've noted, you might choose certain activities to prioritize, at least at first. Then you can expand to assume more of your leadership responsibilities.

Open the "Black Box"

Smart Managing

To help your team develop problem-solving and decision-making skills, show what's happening inside yourself when you attack a problem or weigh a decision.

We've all known managers who are "black boxes": they take in information and spit out solutions or decisions, but don't share their thinking. We can only guess what information they used and how they processed it. It's hard to learn from a black box.

Talk out your thoughts with your employees. Let them know what you're thinking when you're working on a problem or a decision. Invite them to share in your process. Don't be a black box.

Make It an Opportunity

Responsibility can be a heavy burden, and authority can paralyze employees who are unaccustomed to it. Help your teams view their expanded responsibility and authority as opportunity.

For example, instead of telling them, "You're responsible for this project," try something like "You have a chance here to find better ways of handling this situation." They should feel excited by the possibilities, not overwhelmed by expectations.

It's a lot of work, yes, but the results should be well worth your efforts. In fact, you'll likely find that being a new leader is more satisfying, as you help your team members develop their skills and participate more actively in your organization.

Manager's Checklist for Chapter 7

❑ The "old" model of leadership, with the leader at the center of the work group, doesn't work as well now because the several key assumptions on which it was based are less and less valid.

❑ The successful manager now plays six roles: coordinates team activities, advises on problem or opportunity selection, provides resources, coaches on problem solving, assists in implementation, and provides formal and informal recognition.

❑ Leaders get people to do things through any of seven bases of power—position power, personal power, expert power, resource power, reward power, coercive power, or connection power.

❑ When you share your authority with your employees, you can increase your value to the organization by learning how to make the best fit between your new roles and your power bases.

Conducting Team Meetings

N o skill is more critical to the overall success of a team than the ability of its members to conduct focused, effective meetings. Meetings that work are exciting, stimulate active and enthusiastic participation, and result in action.

The Problem with Meetings ...

You know how most people endure meetings as a necessary evil. You're familiar with all the complaints:

- Meetings waste time, energy, and often other resources.
- Meetings are boring.
- Meetings seem to wander or go in circles.
- Meetings seem too driven by what the leader wants: the faster, the better.
- Meetings are too long.
- Meetings are too short.
- Meetings allow too many people to get involved in discussions and decisions.
- Meetings are too often dominated by a few people, while others feel left out.

Those complaints are all over the map. You can't please

everybody, but you can still do a lot to make your team meetings effective, efficient, exciting, and extremely unlikely to generate the types of complaints just listed.

This chapter will concentrate on tactics for meetings. In the self-directed team, sooner or later everyone will probably play a leadership role in the team meeting. So we'll focus on ways to organize, plan, and conduct a meeting. We'll discuss leadership roles and involving team members more actively. We'll also outline a method for structuring and stimulating effective and efficient discussions.

Productive team meetings are perhaps the most important interactions of team members. In fact, they often mean the difference between a successful and unsuccessful team.

We encourage you to share this chapter with your team. After all, the meetings belong to every member of the team. They should be a community effort, with full and active participation.

Meetings and Roles

Throw out strict parliamentary procedures and rules of order. Team meetings demand participation from every member. Each person shares in the responsibility for making each meeting a success.

But just because there's no rigid structure, just

Smart Managing

True or False?

A meeting is an event where minutes are kept and hours are lost.

A meeting is a gathering where people speak up, say nothing, then all disagree.

A meeting is indispensable when you don't want to accomplish anything.

The length of a meeting increases with the square of the number of people present.

If these statements seem true, think about the following observation by Terrence Deal and Allan Kennedy, authors of *Corporate Cultures:* "The form of the meeting is simply a reflection of the culture." It's time for you to help change that culture.

because every team member is encouraged to get involved, that doesn't mean that a meeting is a free-for-all. It's important to encourage freedom, but it's just as important for participants to have a sense of purpose, direction, and accomplishment.

To achieve this, it's good to divide the responsibility for a meeting among several team members. This encourages ownership and cooperation, of course, but it also distributes the work and ensures a sort of "checks and balances" control.

Meeting Leader

The meeting leader is responsible for scheduling the meeting, setting the agenda, sharing that agenda with team members, and handling the logistics—getting the room, providing the necessary equipment and other materials and resources, and inviting any people not on the team. The leader is also responsible for ensuring that the meeting runs according to the schedule and agenda, making assignments, and following up on agreements reached during the meeting.

Facilitator

The facilitator is responsible for the meeting process—the interaction of team members and any other participants. This role allows the meeting leader to focus on what happens before and after the meeting. The facilitator must constantly address the following questions:

CAUTION!

How to Ruin a Meeting

What can ruin a meeting? In *Supervision*, Gregory M. Bounds and John A. Woods list six "meeting killers":

1. Hogging: too much talking by one person
2. Bogging: staying on a subject too long
3. Fogging: avoiding a topic or being vague or defensive
4. Frogging: jumping from topic to topic without any closure on any of them
5. Flogging: attacking a person rather than focusing on that person's input
6. Clogging: slowing down the team by failing to accomplish action items

- Is everybody participating?
- Are we keeping to the agenda and schedule?
- Are participants showing respect for each other?

During brisk flurries of activity, the facilitator should also make sure the scribe and the note-taker are able to keep pace.

Facilitator The person responsible for making it easier for members to participate in the meeting. A good facilitator runs the meeting, not the participants.

Scribe

The scribe records participation, writing out ideas, suggestions, questions, and other input on a flip chart and/or blackboard. This role frees the facilitator to interact more fully with the other participants. The scribe must be able to listen attentively, reword rapidly and accurately if necessary, and write quickly and clearly.

Note-Taker

The note-taker records discussion and decisions. Since the scribe is recording input, the note-taker is relieved of the usual secretarial obligation to jot down every detail. But the note-taker is responsible for keeping track of who makes what points during discussions, what decisions are made, and who will take charge of what actions. The note-taker should be able to write quickly, accurately, and objectively. After the meeting, the note-taker must turn the notes into a report and distribute copies to all participants.

For every meeting, I recommend a leader, a facilitator, a scribe, and a note-taker. It's possible to do without a note-taker, if the scribe can record everything on the chart or the board—although it makes it more difficult to simply walk away with those notes after the meeting! It's also possible, if the meeting is expected to involve

Flip Chart or Blackboard?

Use a chart for specific contributions from participants, for documenting multiple inputs. Use a board for dynamic "rough drafts," when team members are working together to shape and refine an idea.

only moderate discussion, for the facilitator to serve as scribe. But that's a risky assumption, if you've got a good team. The meeting atmosphere can suddenly become more energized than you might expect from the agenda.

Finally, you'll want to alternate roles as much as possible. Don't "type cast" according to personality or writing ability or accurate reporting skills—but don't force roles on team members who are deficient in the requirements. Rotate roles as much as possible, but keep expanding the possibilities by developing your team members.

A good way to do that is through role sharing, which also may allow for a more effective and efficient meeting and perhaps less fatigue. You or the leader may want to choose several facilitators or scribes or note-takers for a meeting, assigning them to cover specific agenda items.

Role sharing can get confusing, especially

The Meeting Leader

As the manager, you're the leader of the team. Should you also be the meeting leader? Not unless it's necessary—and when is that? In the early stages of team development, to model what's expected of the meeting leader. (You'll probably also need to model as facilitator—and maybe even scribe as well.) It may also be a good idea if the agenda includes politically risky topics.

But otherwise, help your people develop, then—as soon as possible—let them run their own meetings.

negotiating the transitions. But there are three key advantages:

1. It provides short periods of on-the-job training for members who need to develop their meeting skills.
2. It allows respite for any members who are overworked with meeting responsibilities.
3. It lets members shed their specific responsibilities for the greater freedom of more active participation.

Guidelines for Effective Team Meetings

Now, how do these roles work together to ensure good meetings? The following guidelines show who, what, when, where, and how. (If you don't know the *why*, go back to the beginning of this chapter and read it again.) Since the responsibilities of the scribe and the note-taker are fairly well delineated, these guidelines indicate only the responsibilities of the leader and the facilitator.

Preparation: In Advance of the Meeting

The leader:

- Develops an agenda, indicating the amount of time for each item.
- Identifies which members will serve as facilitator(s), scribe(s), and note-taker(s), and verifies that they'll be ready and able to assume these roles.
- Identifies any other individual responsibilities—e.g., anybody who should be providing information or reports to the rest of the team—and verifies that they'll be prepared. Asks if they need any special equipment for their presentations.
- Reschedules the meeting if necessary information is unavailable or if actions have been delayed.
- Finalizes the agenda by indicating specific roles and responsibilities.
- Distributes copies of the agenda to team members.
- Schedules the room.
- Arranges for any necessary equipment, other materials, and resources.
- Invites any people who should attend the meeting and are not on the team.
- Anticipates questions and concerns.

Preliminaries: The Start of the Meeting

The leader:

- Explains the purpose and importance of the meeting.
- Reviews the agenda.
- Checks to make sure all participants understand.
- Seeks additional agenda items.
- Sets time limits.

Meeting

The facilitator:

- Makes sure the scribe and the note-taker are ready.
- Begins with a reading of the last meeting's minutes by that

note-taker. Asks for questions, corrections, or clarifications.

- Proceeds through the items on the agenda.
- For each item, asks the person(s) responsible for information or action to report.
- Asks for any additional information or concerns.

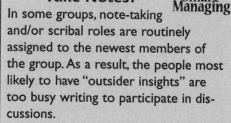

Who Should Take Notes?

Smart Managing

In some groups, note-taking and/or scribal roles are routinely assigned to the newest members of the group. As a result, the people most likely to have "outsider insights" are too busy writing to participate in discussions.

Is that smart management? You be the judge.

- Opens the discussion, if appropriate.
- Defers complex problems or limits discussion of them.
- Asks open questions.
- Encourages balanced participation by limiting those who would dominate and encouraging those who are more reserved.
- Encourages expression of differences of opinion and perspective.
- Solicits ideas, using brainstorming when appropriate. (More on this technique in our discussion of STOP later in this chapter.)
- Pauses and summarizes information, ideas, and alternatives.
- Checks for understanding.

Facilitating Meeting Leadership

Mistake Proofing

It may be difficult for team members to assume the responsibilities of the meeting leader. The following questions may help guide them.

- What is the purpose of this meeting?
- What specific things do we want the team to accomplish?
- What potential problems do we face?
- How should we solve those problems?
- Which members will have specific responsibilities in the meeting?
- What resources—people, equipment, materials, information—will we need?

- Calls for a vote on decisions, working toward consensus whenever possible.
- Gets agreement on actions: what, who, when, how.
- Selects the leader for the next meeting.
- Sets a time and place for the next meeting.
- Identifies information needed for the next meeting and the person(s) responsible.

Follow-up: After the Meeting

The leader:

- Provides support to key players.
- Conducts progress checks on assignments and commitments prior to next meeting.
- Prepares any presentations.
- Works with dominant or reserved members to develop more appropriate group behavior.

It takes a lot of teamwork to conduct good team meetings. But the results should be well worth the efforts.

Norms

Work with your team to develop a set of norms to guide your meetings. Your norms needn't be complicated or cover every possibility. You want to arrive at some basic understanding of how team members should interact during meetings. Shared behavioral norms will guarantee smoother, more productive meetings and give everyone a greater chance to participate actively and to lead.

The norms your team establishes will depend on the members, what they perceive as their needs, and your workplace culture. But here are a few suggestions to consider.

Share ideas. Unless you participate actively in the team meeting and share your ideas, the team can't benefit from what you're thinking. Even

---

TRICKS OF THE TRADE

Encouraging Participation

The facilitator can encourage participation by doing the following:
- Avoid stating his or her ideas until all other members have contributed.
- Use open questions repeatedly.
- Reinforce and praise all input.

members who are shy or have never participated in a meeting have much to contribute.

Listen. It's important to listen to others and understand. Be aware of how much time you talk and how much time you listen in the meeting. Try to balance your participation and spend as much time listening as you do contributing.

Compromise. The guiding principle for working in teams is "Win some, lose some." Consensus means that a decision is acceptable to the team as a whole, not that the decision is perfect. Sometimes what the team wants is not precisely what you want. Unless your principles or values are compromised, go along with the team. All decisions are modified, so you'll usually have further chances to provide input.

Take responsibility. The team is only as good as what it can accomplish. If your team doesn't get much done, it may be, in part, because some members fail to assume their full share of responsibility. When you make a commitment, carry it out. Don't make commitments you can't deliver. If you need help, ask for it.

Handling Common Team Meeting Problems

No matter how good your team may be, no matter what norms you establish for your meetings, problems are inevitable. Those problems won't necessarily undermine your team efforts—if the meeting leader, facilitator, and team members react appropriately to handle the problems as they arise.

Here are some common problems and some suggestions for dealing with them, in the order in which you should try them.

Problem
Negative attitudes, bickering, members unwilling to contribute positively to discussion.
Actions
- Facilitator encourages balanced participation.
- Facilitator stresses the importance of working together to achieve the meeting goals.

- Facilitator asks the whole group for help.
- Leader emphasizes the benefits of meetings in general and the importance of that particular meeting agenda.

Problem
Lack of focus: meetings go on too long without getting to solutions or achieving consensus.

Actions
- Facilitator summarizes differences and agreements.
- Facilitator maintains momentum by using the guidelines.
- Facilitator emphasizes deadlines and a sense of urgency.
- Leader reviews the agenda and stresses time limits.
- Facilitator moves more quickly into making specific assignments, including arranging presentations for upcoming meetings.
- Facilitator ends meeting, deferring the rest of the agenda for the next meeting.

Problem
Disruptive individuals (either positive or negative).

Actions
- Facilitator listens to their concerns and integrates them into the plans, for the current meeting or subsequent meetings, as appropriate.
- Facilitator reminds the members of the importance of following the agenda or of properly amending it.
- Other members use group pressure to help their disruptive teammates adhere to meeting norms.
- Manager meets with the disruptive members outside the meeting to coach on meeting behavior.
- Manager meets with the disruptive members outside the meeting to involve them in a project of interest.
- Manager uses the performance appraisal system to set meeting behavior goals.

Problem
Silence or little participation during meetings.

Actions
- Facilitator becomes more animated, asks more probing questions.

- Facilitator assigns agenda items to individuals or pairs to prepare for the next meeting, with each assuming the responsibility of serving as facilitator for that particular agenda item.
- Leaders encourage members presenting reports to use more visual aids.
- Leaders plan more controversial topics for discussion.
- Manager encourages more active participation by rotating the roles of meeting leader and facilitator.
- Manager suggests that team members sit in with more active teams.
- Manager empowers team with more important decision responsibilities.

Problem

Lack of commitment: members don't follow up on assignments or actions as agreed.

Actions

- Facilitator asks for reasons for lack of action, listens to concerns and disagreements.
- Facilitator re-emphasizes the purpose and importance of meetings and assignments as essential parts of teamwork.
- Facilitator sets and stresses deadlines and emphasizes agreement when making assignments.
- Leaders correct behaviors by properly and more fully preparing for meetings.
- Facilitator interrupts agenda to encourage team to help identify goals of greater interest, to consider with the manager.

Problem

Members show anger toward facilitator, meeting leader, and/or manager.

Actions

Whoever is the focus of the anger takes the following actions:

- Avoids confrontation.
- Uses reflecting skills.
- Listens without commenting.
- Expresses understanding for concerns.

- Asks for further concerns.
- Reminds the team that everyone is learning new skills.
- Says, "I hear you and I'll do my best."

Facilitator returns to the agenda to continue the meeting.

Problem

Late arrivals.

Actions

- Facilitator asks what made them late.
- Facilitator emphasizes the necessity of starting on time.
- Facilitator starts without full team in attendance.
- Leader schedules meeting at start of work day.

What You Should Do as Manager

Although the problems just discussed involve behavior during meetings, their causes can generally be found outside the meeting—in planning and in follow-up. Although meeting leaders are responsible for planning and follow-up for specific meetings, you as team manager should be aware of any need to ensure continuity in those areas and to help reinforce the importance of commitment and preparation for all members.

If behavioral problems continue to affect meetings, it may be wise to schedule a meeting to discuss team responsibilities and further develop norms for your team meetings. You may also want to be more careful in assigning the roles of meeting leader and facilitator, at least until meetings improve.

As I stated at the beginning of this chapter, the ability to conduct focused, effective meetings is the skill most critical to the success of teams.

Problem-Solving Techniques for Meetings

Most effective teams are also good problem-solvers. As they become more self-sufficient, teams develop a common language of problem solving that helps them focus on problems without getting bogged down or losing sight of their objective.

(I'm using the term "problem solving" here to refer generally to any attempt to improve a certain situation, whether by coming up with a solution to a problem, or trying to take advantage of an opportunity—which would be a real problem only if you don't find ways to benefit.)

There are many models of problem solving. Most emphasize a systematic approach that consists of three essentials:

- Define the nature of the problem.
- Identify the potential causes.
- Seek solutions.

Unfortunately, many problem-solving techniques prove too complicated for a lot of situations. When you need to work efficiently, when quick analysis and fast decisions are required, teams need a process that provides action plans right away.

I recommend a practical process called STOP, which stands for *Situation-Target-Options-Plan.* Using STOP, a team can approach many problems systematically and involve all members in developing action plans in a minimum of time.

Problem solving can take place in many ways. It can be done alone, in the privacy of your work area as you mentally review a checklist of what went wrong with a piece of equipment or a process. It can happen in an air-conditioned conference room between executives using overheads and slide presentations. It can take place in a lunchroom where the team brainstorms causes for a line breakdown. It can occur spontaneously at the site of the problem with the two or three people responsible for a process putting their heads together, diagnosing the problem, and suggesting three or four possible solutions. It can even be in a conference room with computer equipment humming, VDT screens calling up figures or diagrams, and engineers testing different designs or theories.

Where and *when* problem solving takes place is of less importance than *how* it takes place. To be effective, problem solving should balance the *creative* and the *analytical.*

That balance is not necessarily constant: sometimes the analytical predominates, sometimes the creative. But a good balance of creative and analytical ensures better solutions.

The Four Parts of STOP

STOP can help maintain that balance of creative and analytical while providing a common language that focuses the team.

STOP combines brainstorming, the most useful creative problem-solving tool, with other methods, some of which require analysis and research.

Situation

Purpose: To identify the problem and brainstorm when, where, and how often it occurs. If you're unsure of the cause or causes of a problem, determine the most likely ones first.

Technique: Brainstorming

Target

Purpose: To describe what the process would look like if the problem were suddenly eliminated. Set a goal based on your vision of a perfect situation.

Technique: SMART Goal Setting

Options

Purpose: To generate creative ideas that will eliminate problems and bring about the vision.

Technique: Brainstorming

Plan

Purpose: To prioritize the ideas according to the *effort* it will take to implement them and their overall *impact* on the problem. Then, you make an action plan for the best idea or ideas.

Technique: Effort-Impact Action Planning

Situation: Brainstorming

Brainstorming is the most useful problem-solving technique. But it takes practice to become really proficient. Success in brainstorming is based on the principle that those doing the work are best qualified to solve its problems. It also assumes that people are creative, able to come up with lots of ideas if given the chance, and able to build on the ideas of others to generate solutions to problems.

Brainstorming works best in groups of five to eight people, although it can often be done with as few as three or even more than twelve people. Everyone should participate, as somebody writes down the ideas generated. (If you assign the meeting roles discussed earlier in this chapter, that "somebody" would probably be the scribe, but possibly the notetaker.) In general, brainstorming sessions are conducted during team meetings, apart from work distractions.

Conducting a Brainstorming Session

Although there's no one way to run a brainstorming session, certain guidelines have proven helpful. Follow these guidelines while you become familiar with brainstorming. Then develop whatever procedures bring out the best in your team.

In the STOP method, you use brainstorming twice:

- In the Situation phase, to better understand your problem by examining it from all perspectives and bringing out all aspects of your situation.
- In the Options phase, to generate possible solutions to your problem, to put all your options on the table.

The following description of the brainstorming procedure applies to both Situation and Options phases.

1. Select the theme or project area to be your focus. Make sure everybody understands the focus. If possible, communicate your focus before the meeting.
2. Allow a few moments for everyone to think a little and collect their thoughts before beginning the interaction.
3. Set a time limit. A sense of urgency can further stimulate contributions. Also, there's nothing more boring than a brainstorming session that goes on too long.
4. Appoint a facilitator to supervise the process and a fast-writing scribe who can record ideas on the board or flip chart. This keeps all ideas out in front of the team and allows members to build on each other's ideas.
5. Group your ideas into categories. This helps eliminate duplicate ideas and makes it easier to select final ideas.
6. Make sure that everybody understands all of the ideas suggested.
7. Prioritize your ideas. If you're defining a problem (Situation), you should prioritize

Let Them Think First

Some team members may find it hard to speak in public, or they may be influenced or intimidated by the more vocal members of the group. To help them get started, the facilitator should allow a few minutes for everyone to write ideas on a piece of paper. Then, when the brainstorming starts, everyone will be prepared to speak.

Smart Managing

in terms of the importance of the ideas. If you're generating ideas (Options), you'll want to prioritize in terms of many issues. (That's the purpose of the Plan phase and the Effort-Impact Matrix, as we'll see shortly.)

Target: SMART Goal Setting

In the STOP method, the target is a goal that generally describes what results you expect from your solutions.

While it's perfectly OK to describe the target in words, numbers help. A numerical target is doubly useful, because it can provide you with a clear criterion to use twice—now, in assessing the probability of success for any suggested solutions and later, in evaluating the results of the solution you choose.

One procedure for setting your target is SMART, an acronym that represents the five aspects of a good goal.

SMART Goals

Specific
Be as specific as possible. For example, "Fred doesn't talk to Mary" is better than "There are communication problems in department X."

Measurable
Be quantitative whenever possible. If you can express a problem quantitatively, you've got a better chance of solving it. For example, "increase productivity by 5%" is better than "work harder."

Agreed Upon
Be sure the whole team is behind your target. Is there consensus that this is the problem you should all focus your time and effort on?

TOOLS

Affinity Diagrams

A handy brainstorming technique is affinity diagramming—brainstorming in categories.

Write your topic on the board and begin brainstorming. With the first idea, draw a line from the topic off to one side and create a category. Then brainstorm in that category or create another. When you have several categories, the team will move at random from one to another.

An affinity diagram sorts your ideas into categories. You can then address these categories individually or group them.

Reachable or Realistic

Be sure your target is practical. Can the team really solve this problem or complete this project? Or has it bitten off more than it can chew?

Time-Bound

Be on a schedule if possible. It's a hard fact of life: things that have deadlines are more likely to get done. Try to put a sense of urgency into your target.

Options: Brainstorming

The next phase is to generate suggestions for solving the problem you defined in the Situation phase, in terms of the goal you defined in the Target phase. Use brainstorming to explore your options, emphasizing open and creative thinking.

As I mentioned in Chapter 4, the word "brainstorm" was originally used for a sudden and violent disturbance in the brain that could produce clever or crazy ideas. But those ideas come most easily when you remember that the only "rule" of brainstorming is to refrain from discussing or judging any ideas. Keep brainstorming open, free, and positive, and you're most likely to maximize the creativity of your team.

Greenlighting

If some members dominate while others fail to get involved, you might try greenlighting.

Greenlighting is a brainstorming technique that involves all group members equally. Move around the table and allow each person a moment to share his or her idea. If he or she has none, pass to the next person. Go around the table as many times as it takes to get all the ideas out.

Plan: Effort-Impact Action Planning

In the first three phases of the STOP method, you've explored your problem (Situation), determined your goal (Target), and generated a lot of ideas (Options). In the final phase, to go from ideas to action, you need to make some important choices.

Selecting from among a list of *possible* options involves thinking through all the business issues that impact your idea.

Does the idea make sense from the basis of cost, time to implement, amount of effort needed to get it started?

Many factors go into making an astute business decision. One way to capture these factors is by using an Effort-Impact Matrix. This matrix allows you to quantify the ideas generated by your brainstorming in terms of two criteria. "Effort" can be defined as the amount of *regular work time, money, overtime, meeting time, or difficulty* involved in implementing an idea. "Impact" means the *overall effectiveness* of the idea.

> **⚠ CAUTION!**
>
> **TSOP (Sometimes)**
> No method works in all circumstances, at least not without some adaptations. The STOP method puts Situation before Target. But you may want to set your target first, to focus your brainstorming more than you would with just a theme or project area. This would probably be the best approach if a specific goal is imposed on the team.

The Effort-Impact Matrix (Figure 8-1) allows the team to position each idea relative to the amount of effort needed to implement it and its expected impact. When deciding where to place an idea, think in terms of the effort continuum and the impact continuum, rather than the four quadrants. In other words, think of the matrix as a graph that shows degrees of effort and impact, not as four categories.

Once you've placed all your options all over the matrix, you're ready to select. In general, those ideas that require *little effort* while having *great impact* are winners. But if your team is new to problem solving, you may want to try low-effort and low-impact ideas, especially if you have few resources or little time. Smaller solutions allow a team to build expertise, avoid excessive complexity, and minimize resource use.

So, your team selects one of the options, the solution that seems most appropriate to your situation, target, and effort-impact considerations. Now what?

You develop an action plan, that's what! You define roles, responsibilities, and schedules. Work together, building agreement and commitment. Make sure your action plan is complete before you try to take any action.

Action Plan

The action plan consists of three points and a progress check:

What: the actions
1. Set a specific goal.
2. Agree on first steps.
3. Prioritize the sequence of those steps.

Who: the persons responsible
1. Involve everyone in the actions.
2. Relate the actions to regular schedules or work plans.
3. Involve others not on the team.

When: the time frame
1. Determine start and stop points.
2. Set clear deadlines.

> **Effort and Impact**
> "Effort" is the amount of *work time* (regular or overtime), *meeting time, money,* or *difficulty* involved in implementing an idea. "Impact" is the *overall effectiveness* of the idea in solving the problem.

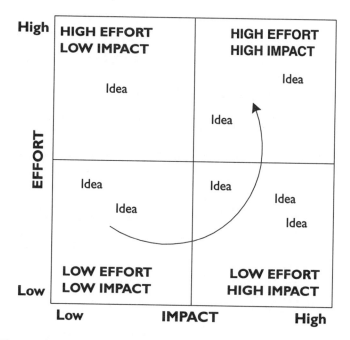

Figure 8-1. Effort-impact matrix

3. Agree to meet to discuss delays.

4. Have a contingency plan.

Progress check: means of assessing progress

1. Use monitoring tools at checkpoints.

2. Hold regular status meetings.

3. Monitor results, not just activity.

There you have it—the basics of the STOP method, a practical process teams can use to deal with problems systematically, to move into action effectively and efficiently. Using STOP, all team members can work together to develop action plans in a minimum of time.

Manager's Checklist for Chapter 8

❑ No ability is more crucial to the overall success of a team than the ability of its members to conduct focused, effective meetings that are exciting, stimulate active and enthusiastic participation, and result in action.

❑ Divide the responsibility for a meeting among several team members—meeting leader, facilitator, scribe, and notetaker. This encourages ownership and cooperation, distributes the work, and ensures a balance of control.

❑ Play a role in meetings, but only as necessary.

❑ Teach your team members how to approach problems systematically and develop action plans efficiently using a process called STOP—*Situation-Target-Options-Plan.*

❑ To maintain control of meetings, get your team members to develop a set of guidelines for meetings and commit to following them.

❑ When meetings fail, it's usually from a lack of planning, rather than a lack of control during the meeting.

Coaching Teams and Team Members

The most effective way to empower a team and help the members develop is through coaching. In this chapter, I'll describe the principles of coaching and how to work with individual team members and with teams as a whole.

Who coaches? You, of course. But also the team members coach each other—and maybe occasionally you! This chapter is intended primarily for you, because as manager of the team you have the greatest coaching responsibilities. But it's also intended for your team members, who aren't just employees in the same work area, but teammates devoted to doing whatever they can to become better together.

Since anybody can provide coaching (not just the manager!) and anybody can benefit from coaching (even the manager!), I'm going to use two terms to refer to those two roles, "coach" and "player." These terms fit the concept of teams,

| **Coach** Somebody who provides training, support, encouragement, correction, and positive reinforcement to help individuals or members of a team develop their potential and feel better about themselves. A little idealistic? Maybe. But why not? That all depends on you. |

Key Term

borrowed from sports, and suggest a collaborative relationship between two peers, with one able to help the other in a particular situation.

Of course, because you as manager are accountable for your employees to your manager, we need to emphasize specifics of coaching that apply to you alone and the expectations imposed on you by your title. Also, because you as manager hold a position of authority above your employees, we need to emphasize ways to establish a relationship that's less manager-employee, even if it can't be truly peer-peer.

The Basics of Coaching

If we were to create a job description for "Coach," what would it include? What activities would it entail? What sense of purpose would it convey?

We could start by stating that a coach teaches and trains. That involves telling, showing, observing, asking, supporting, and providing feedback—both correction and positive reinforcement. Coaching may focus on job knowledge and skills, social behaviors, teamwork, leadership—whatever a player needs to improve.

That brings us to the purposes of coaching. The coach has two goals: to help the players develop and to improve work performance. Which goal is more important? That depends on the situation, on the relative priorities that you assign to the following according to the specific circumstances:

- the player
- the activity
- the specific task or behavior
- the degree of responsibility
- the importance of the effects, actual or potential
- the gap between performance and expectations

That's a lot of priorities to balance. But nobody promised that coaching would be easy!

Usually the development purpose is part of the performance purpose, and the two are more or less in alignment. When that's the case, coaching is simplified—although it still takes skills, savvy, and sensitivity.

OK, so much for a general overview. Let's get into specifics. We can't cover every instance in which coaching would be beneficial, so we'll focus on the three most important areas: job performance, teamwork, and leadership.

Job Performance

Coaching job performance can be divided into three purposes: to develop basic skills, to correct problems, and to improve performance. There are two basic differences among these purposes.

The first difference, of course, is the goal. You help your players develop basic skills so they can do the job. You correct problems to help your players meet the standards. You improve performance to raise those standards and/or to help your players expand their involvement and responsibilities. You may not distinguish much among skills training, correcting problems, and improving performance, especially if you're a proponent of continuous quality improvement or similar approaches to business. They're different areas of a single continuum—and the difference shrinks as you coach.

The second difference may be more significant in practice. You provide skills training when any of your players begins a new task—as soon as possible, with one or with several, depending on their needs. You improve performance any time your players are ready; you can work on it with individuals or as a team. But you correct problems only when they arise— and always privately, one on one with the player in question. We all have memories of coaches who criticized players in public: that's coaching to *punish*, not to *correct and improve*.

Training for Skills

This is the simplest type of coaching. In fact, you may share this area of coaching, if your organization has trainers. Also, if you hire people with the minimal skills to do the job, you may not need to provide much skills training, at least not initially.

Whatever training your players require, you should be able to provide it more effectively if you follow these guidelines.

Guidelines for Coaching
1. Prepare the player.
- Assess the player's skills, preferably by asking him or her to do tasks while you observe. Be sensitive, especially if the player is new to your organization, your area, or your team.
- Ask questions as necessary.
- Discuss the skills the player needs, reviewing details of the demonstrated performance.
- Agree on the goals for your training.

2. Create a positive atmosphere.
- Reassure the player about his or her potential.
- Share any problems you experienced in acquiring the skills in question.
- Seek and listen to the player's concerns.
- Provide a safety net for taking risks. Help the player feel comfortable with the unfamiliar and difficult.
- Communicate your high expectations.

3. Demonstrate or describe the desired performance.
- Work from the simple to the complex.
- Review the desired performance, using examples of acceptable and unacceptable performance.
- Explain the key steps in achieving the goal.
- Demonstrate the desired performance and/or role-play correct behaviors.
- Have the player repeat the instructions back to you.

4. Have the player perform the operation.
- Ensure a low-risk setting for practice.
- Check for any last-minute concerns or questions.
- Videotape the performance for detailed follow-up coaching.
- Provide all the resources and supplies necessary.
- Keep a low profile while the player is practicing the new skills or behaviors.
- Avoid body language or words that could interfere with practice. Be quietly positive and supportive.

5. Follow up.

- Praise the player for his or her efforts and congratulate him or her on the results achieved.
- Provide timely, detailed feedback.
- Make sure the player has plans for continued practice.
- Schedule additional coaching as needed.
- Ask for suggestions to improve your coaching skills. This is the best time, since the player is most likely to remember specifics—and because there are psychological benefits for the player who can switch roles and become the coach, if only briefly.

Correcting Problems

No matter how well you train your players, no matter how hard your players may try, problems are inevitable. In fact, the more you empower your players, the more likely they are to make mistakes. It's the business equivalent of that athletic truism—"No pain, no gain."

How can you minimize the negative effects of mistakes and maximize the positive? I recommend the following guidelines in coaching team members in situations that involve correcting problems.

Guidelines for Correcting Performance Problems

- Review the problem with the player and discuss its importance.
- Express your personal concern about the situation.
- Discuss significant background information.

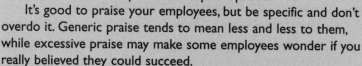

Too Much of a Good Thing

You can't have too much of a good thing—usually. There's at least one important exception: praise.

It's good to praise your employees, but be specific and don't overdo it. Generic praise tends to mean less and less to them, while excessive praise may make some employees wonder if you really believed they could succeed.

Be sensitive to their reactions. If an individual seems more embarrassed than pleased, you may want to back off a little. Otherwise, it's better to praise too much than too little.

- Listen to the player's perspective and repeat it to clarify and understand.
- Seek solutions and discuss alternatives.
- Agree on follow-up actions.
- Assure the player of your support by expressing high expectations.

Nobody can guarantee that any guidelines will produce optimum results. But you certainly boost your chances if you're open, positive, supportive, and share your belief that we learn and improve through our problems.

Smart Managing

When an Error Occurs...

1. Acknowledge it.
2. Correct it.
3. Learn from it.
4. Continue.

If you follow this procedure, *errors* will never become *failures*.

Providing Feedback

To provide effective feedback, you must always remember to balance structure and support. Here are some criteria that can help make feedback effective:

Desired by the player: The player is ready and willing to accept feedback and to make changes to improve.

Timely: The feedback is provided at the right time, shortly after the need is perceived and when corrective action can be taken.

Straightforward: The coach provides the feedback orally and in person, not over the phone, in writing, or through a third person.

MISTAKE PROOFING

A Quote to Note

"Success and failure. We think of them as opposites, but they're really not. They're companions—the hero and the sidekick."
—Lawrence Shames

The biggest mistake may well be to forget this fundamental truth.

Behavioral: The feedback addresses specific actions.

Improvement-Based: The feedback is based on improvement, not feelings. It should focus on the work, set standards and organizational goals.

Actionable: The feedback aims at actions within the player's ability.

Improving Performance

This is when coaching can really be exciting and fun. Your players are performing up to standards and feeling good. Now you can help them raise those standards and enlarge their "3-C zone"—competence, confidence, and comfort.

Maybe the organization would like to boost productivity or increase efficiency. Maybe the tasks are changing. Or maybe you just feel that some or all of your players are ready to take their work to a higher level.

It can be exciting and fun for you, as their manager and coach. But your players won't necessarily be enthusiastic about expanding that zone— at least not at first. After all, you're encouraging them to take more chances and risk having problems and making mistakes.

> **A Riddle**
>
> What is the shortest word in the English language that contains the letters A, B, C, D, E, and F? Answer: feedback.
>
> That bit of trivia may help remind you that feedback is an essential element of good communication, as basic as A, B, C (and D, E, and F).

Smart Managing

The following guidelines should help you capitalize on opportunities to improve and to help your players feel motivated by the challenge and eager to continue developing their abilities and assuming greater responsibilities.

Raising Expectations

- Describe the situation, whether improvement is needed or just possible.
- Assure the player that current performance is good, but you'd like to work on improving it.
- Specify the differences between what's being done now and what should or can be done differently.
- Listen to any concerns and questions the player might have.
- Discuss any concerns or questions—including any you might want to add.

- Agree on an action plan.
- Agree on goals and a follow-up procedure.
- Thank the player and express your support.

Finally, remember that in raising your expectations you're inviting problems and mistakes. Don't be afraid, but don't assume that all will go well. Remember the words of Benjamin Franklin, "By failing to prepare, you are preparing to fail."

Developing Team Players

Do you remember those report cards back in elementary school? Among the various criteria the teachers used was that standard, "Works and plays well with others." Now, years later, we may have forgotten about all the other criteria, but that one standard remains. It's important how we all work and play with others on the job, especially in teams.

What makes a good work team player? What skills, behaviors, and characteristics or personality traits do you value most and want to develop in your employees?

If you asked 100 managers that question, you might get 100 answers. But those managers would probably agree on most if not all of the following skills, behaviors, and characteristics—although not necessarily in any specific order.

The ideal work team player:

- Assumes responsibility
- Likes to help others
- Cooperates and collaborates
- Communicates well—listening and reading as well as speaking and writing
- Communicates appropriately—recognizes the need to maintain connections with others
- Grasps and keeps in mind the big picture
- Feels and shows team spirit
- Exudes a positive attitude
- Is interested in improving
- Appreciates differences among people
- Is reliable

- Trusts teammates and manager
- Shows respect for others
- Handles conflicts appropriately
- Has a healthy sense of self-esteem—neither arrogant nor servile
- Commits to work and to teammates and manager
- Exercises critical ability, reasons, analyzes
- Is loyal
- Is empathetic
- Can offer criticism constructively and sensitively
- Can appreciate criticism—not just tolerate or accept it, but benefit from it

That's a long list—and it could easily be a little longer. I encourage you to return to this list from time to time as you work with teams. You'll likely want to add some skills, behaviors, or characteristics. (Friendly? Sense of humor? High energy? Patient? Kind?)

Better yet, post a copy of this list on your office wall, to remind you of what you want to develop in your players. Express your appreciation of these qualities whenever possible. That's the easiest, most basic step in coaching team players.

Developing Leaders

How do you train team members to be leaders? That's a trick question—you've been training them by your example. So, if you've been a good model, you can simply encourage them to take initiative and support them in their efforts. If not, well, it's time to work on being a better leader yourself.

General Development

When you allow members of your team to assume greater responsibilities, to lead their teammates, how do you expect them to do so? What powers should they be able to tap?

Think about that question for a moment—because it's certainly on the mind of any employee expected to exercise any leadership. Do you remember the seven bases of power from Chapter 7? Which of those seven are most appropriate for your employees to use as they develop their leadership?

Position power? Only as a last resort, because this power tends to be divisive on a team.

Personal power? The most effective, although success in using this power base will vary considerably according to individual people skills.

Expert power? Often a very strong base, particularly when the team is composed of employees with quite different areas of expertise—technical experience, work experience, maturity, or problem-solving ability. A possible downside: team members can get into leadership ruts so they're less likely to show leadership initiative in areas beyond their particular expertise.

Resource power? Similar to position power in a team context, because the resource will generally come through you, as manager and team leader.

Reward power? Potentially like resource power and position power, if the rewards come through you, the manager. But an effective power if team members develop informal rewards, even just expressing their appreciation in simple ways.

Coercive power? Worse than position power. Dangerous power for anyone in a leadership position, but especially destructive in a team context.

Connection power? To be avoided, at least in terms of traditional connections to people in greater power. A great source of potential power if the connections are with other teams in the organization or similar teams in other organizations.

The question of appropriate and effective power is difficult for any *leader.* But it's even more difficult for *employees* who are unaccustomed to acting as leaders. After all, even if you've been a model leader, your employees have probably been exposed to bad leadership styles and behaviors.

You may want to devote part of a team meeting to discussing the seven sources of power. Don't tell your people what powers to use or not to use. Each of them should make that decision alone. All you want to do is discuss advantages and disadvantages, and encourage them to think about power and how it can be used—or abused.

Assignments and Projects

The first question here should not be "How can I help members of my team show leadership on assignments and projects?" That's the second question, which depends on the first—"Who determined which employees would be in charge of which assignment and which projects?" In other words, who's leading those employees?

The answer to that question determines how you should help your employees handle assignments and projects.

If an employee is in charge of something because of you, then it's OK to proceed to the second question—"How can I help members of my team show leadership on assignments and projects?" The best answer: encourage them to come discuss their thoughts with you or share their progress. Show them you're confident and very interested. Then it's up to them to do the rest, to feel comfortable about seeking help from you.

But if an employee is in charge of something because of a teammate—most likely a meeting leader or facilitator—then you just forget about that question of helping. Allow your employees to help each other, to work things out together, to solve any problems on their own. And trust them to

---

A Mug and A Prayer

TRICKS OF THE TRADE

A colleague who enjoyed considerable success with empowering his team once shared his simple secret with me. Whenever he felt anxious or frustrated, he told me, he'd simply close his office door and hold his favorite coffee mug with both hands for a few moments.

I thought he was crazy—until he showed me the mug. On it was written that old, familiar prayer: "God grant me the serenity to accept the things I cannot change, the courage to change the things I can, and the wisdom to know the difference."

That, he noted, was the essence of life for the empowering manager.

let you know if they'd like any help from you.

What if the employee just took the initiative for a project or an assignment? Well, then, congratulations! You've got somebody showing leadership there. So, you simply express your appreciation to that employee and invite him or her to come talk with you about it at any time. A team manager often helps most by just showing trust and exercising a little patience.

Meeting Roles

The leadership involved in the roles needed to run team meetings—meeting leader, facilitator, scribe, and note-taker— imposes certain requirements on team members, as we discussed in Chapter 8. Of course, you've already discussed these roles in a team meeting, so every member understands what each role entails. The roles are fairly well defined and they depend on close collaboration and a shared understanding of role responsibilities and how they fit together.

That's why I offer the following coaching guidelines, so you can help your employees serve the team in these four roles. The bottom line: the best way to support your employees when they serve as leaders is to show your respect for the ways in which they exercise their leadership.

Before the Meeting

- Set a time and place for you and the meeting leader to meet to discuss the agenda. Make sure that he or she will prepare the agenda before meeting with you.
- Ask the meeting leader to review the agenda with you. You might also want to briefly discuss each item, to better prepare for the meeting.
- Determine if the agenda is realistic for the meeting. If you have any concerns, ask questions, from open to more specific. But try to avoid making agenda decisions: that's meddling.
- Ask the team leader if he or she anticipates any problems. If so, ask about how he or she plans to deal with them.
- Ask what other preparations he or she has made. Ask questions, if you have concerns, but don't provide answers.

- Find out who will be facilitator, scribe, and note-taker. It's up to the meeting leader to help those teammates be ready for their roles, but you may want to ask questions if you have any specific concerns.
- Check that the meeting leader has taken care of logistics—scheduling a room and arranging for flip chart, audio-visual equipment, etc.
- Determine whether or not you'll attend and, if so, what your role will be, if any. (It's probably best for you to be only an observer, to let the meeting leader and facilitator run things.)
- Ask when the meeting leader will get the agenda out to the other team members. (They should already know the time and place, decided at the end of the previous meeting, but should be allowed sufficient opportunity to think about the items on the agenda.)

During the Meeting

- Allow the meeting leader and the facilitator to run the meeting. Play any assigned role or simply observe.
- Support the meeting leader as needed—if he or she requests your help.

When to Intervene   CAUTION!

As a manager, you have considerable power. But as team leader and coach, you want to empower your team members. Be careful about stepping in when problems arise during a meeting.

In deciding whether to intervene, consider the following questions:

- Is the meeting leader asking for help and is it needed?
- Is the team leader saying or doing something that should be challenged?
- Would your knowledge, experience, or opinion measurably improve the situation?
- Can you solve the problem with a simple "Yes" or "No"?
- Is a technique or method being used incorrectly?
- Is something being planned that's illegal, unethical, or against policy unknown to the team?
- Do you have information that would measurably benefit the team at this time?

- If any team members (other than the meeting leader) address any questions to you, direct them to the meeting leader. You should answer only if the leader asks you to.
- Note participation levels and any problems. Also note anything about the roles played by the meeting leader, facilitator, or scribe to discuss later in one-on-one meetings.
- If you find it necessary to intervene, signal subtly to the facilitator.

After the Meeting
  (with meeting leader)
- Schedule to meet with the meeting leader.
- Ask open questions about how he or she would evaluate the meeting's effectiveness.
- Ask about what he or she would consider high points and areas of concern. Then ask how he or she would improve on those areas of concern.
- Indicate what you'd consider high points and areas of concern. Get his or her thoughts about your assessment. Then ask how he or she would improve on those areas of concern.
- Review the agenda to determine whether it worked as planned.
- Review team participation and any specific, unexpected behaviors.
- Discuss any help or support the team needs.
  (with facilitator)
- Schedule a time and place to meet with the facilitator.
- Ask open questions about how he or she would evaluate his or her performance as facilitator. What worked well? What didn't work? How could he or she have improved the structure and flow of the meeting and the interaction of the participants?
- Offer any comments on the performance and any suggestions for improvement in that role.
- Review team participation and any specific, unexpected behaviors.
- Discuss any help or support the team needs.

The follow-up meetings with the meeting leader and the facilitator should focus on the future, on ways to improve team meetings. If you note recurrent problems or common concerns, you may decide to address them in a team meeting.

So much for the meeting leader and the facilitator—the major roles in team meetings. What about the scribe and the note-taker? Since these roles are much more limited, there are usually few problems with either role.

Any concerns about the scribe should be discussed during your follow-up meeting with the facilitator. If the two of you agree on some aspect of the scribe's performance that could be improved, ask the facilitator to discuss them with the scribe. Of course, some problems are handled naturally during the course of the meeting. If, for example, a scribe writes illegibly or neglects to record a contribution, team members should quickly but sensitively correct the problem.

It's different with the role of note-taker. Any problems are likely to be discovered only when he or she writes and distributes the minutes of the meeting. At that point, if there are any areas of concern, they're beyond the "jurisdiction" of the meeting leader, so it's best for you to handle them yourself.

It might be just a matter of organizing and writing skills, so you might offer some suggestions—assuming that your own organizing and writing skills are at least adequate! If the note-taker had problems keeping up with the flow of the meeting, encourage him or her to signal to the facilitator whenever the flow becomes a problem. (A simple gesture works best.) Maybe the note-taker had difficulties deciding what to record. If so, ask him or her to sit down with the meeting leader the next time, just after the meeting, to discuss what should be included in the meeting minutes.

What if a team member is dissatisfied with his or her performance of a meeting role and wants another chance right away? If the role was meeting leader, advise him or her to volunteer for that role at the end of the next meeting. If the role was facilitator, scribe, or note-taker, suggest that he or she ask the new meeting leader, who's responsible for assigning those three supporting roles for the next meeting. But make sure that such requests don't excessively disrupt your regular rotation of roles. Every member of the team should have about the same opportunity to play each of the four meeting roles.

You may be wondering about the time and energy you'll be spending in discussions with meeting leaders, facilitators, scribes, and note-takers. Consider it an investment in leadership development and team empowerment. Like any investment, it should pay off—and return benefits. After a while, these meetings might take no more than five or ten minutes. Also, keep an open mind: you might just learn a few things about your employees ... and about leadership!

Coaching from a Distance

Our discussion of coaching has implicitly assumed that you're around your players to observe their job performance, social behaviors, and teamwork. But one of the advantages of a team environment and appropriate development and coaching is that employees need less close supervision. (In fact, your leadership shows less in what happens when you're *there* than in what happens when you're *not* there.)

Well, then how do you know what and how your employees are doing so you can coach them?

You do *unobserved coaching* or coaching from a distance, a technique useful for gathering information if you're not present when and where they're doing their jobs or involved in team meetings, projects, or assignments. It's simple, but not necessarily natural for most managers. The traditional ways of checking on employees may not be best for teams.

Here's a procedure for finding out about how a player has handled or is handling a given situation—a job, a team meeting, a project, or an assignment.

- Ask the player to list the high points of the situation, with examples. ("What do you feel were the most important aspects? Give me some examples. Why would these be important?")

- Ask the player to describe any problem areas and provide examples. ("Did you have any problems? What kinds? Any specific problems? Why did these problems come up, in your opinion?")
- Ask the player to describe his or her actions and the consequences. ("What did you do? Then what happened?")
- Praise actions that you consider appropriate. ("Good idea to do ...! That was smart. It seems like an appropriate way to handle the situation.")
- Show support for tough judgment calls. ("That was a difficult situation, with some hard choices.")
- Probe and support corrective actions. ("What did you do to deal with the problems? I'm glad you tried to handle them. I knew I could count on you to do your best.")
- Probe for more appropriate actions. ("Now that you've had a little time to think about it, what could you have done to handle the situation a little better?")
- If necessary, role-play the situation to practice more appropriate behaviors. ("OK, let's try this. Let's go back and relive the situation. Only I'll be you and you be ....")

The two most important things to keep in mind about coaching from a distance are:

- **You were not there.** It's always easier when you're not actually involved in the action to second-guess any decisions, especially when they don't work out perfectly.
- **You're not the player.** You're the coach. Sure, you probably could have handled the situation better; you've got more experience, more knowledge, superior skills, and possibly greater natural abilities. But until scientists are able to clone dozens of you, your job is to help your employees develop, not to wish you could do everything.

How can you know if you're succeeding at coaching from a distance? Well, if your employees try to avoid you, then you're failing. But if they're eager to talk with you, even if things didn't work out very well—congratulations, coach!

Players as Coaches

As we stated early in this chapter, every member of the team is responsible for coaching his or her teammates as appropriate—and for coaching you, their manager and head coach.

Encourage your employees to recognize the synergy of working together and helping each other develop. This is a natural instinct: kids tend to share what they know how to do, helping their friends acquire knowledge and skills. People don't learn how to do that: it just happens. Unfortunately, we all seem to lose that natural tendency by the time we enter the world of work.

Working as a team means more than just employees doing work together. It means teammates helping each other, not just to do the work, but to do it better, more easily, more efficiently.

So, if you've got only one coach on your team, maybe you really don't have a team yet.

Recognition

As I noted in Chapter 7, one of the six new leadership roles is to provide formal and informal recognition for your employees. A good manager knows that's perhaps the most important yet often neglected part of the coaching process.

When you recognize the efforts and accomplishments of your players, you're getting at least four benefits:

For Example

High-Output Questions

The best questions to ask, especially for coaching at a distance, are questions that get information rather than provide guidance. These are "high-output" questions. For example:
- What have you done so far?
- How has it worked?
- Who have you talked with about this?
- What else are you doing?
- Have you considered any other options?
- Have we ever had this problem?

These questions are specific in their scope, yet open to whatever answer your employee wants to provide.

1. The player receiving the recognition feels appreciated and a greater sense of motivation.
2. Teammates and other employees generally feel motivated to work harder and smarter.
3. The celebration helps support team spirit and bolster morale.
4. The recognition shows you're a manager who believes in your employees, in the psychological and social dimensions of human activities.

The ways in which we recognize our team players run the gamut from formal, organizational awards (or even state, regional, national, and international awards) to the very informal, casual displays of acknowledgment and appreciation.

Formal recognition can be a powerful incentive, but in most organizations it happens too infrequently to have a great impact on performance. As manager, you should find various ways to recognize your employees.

In *Supervision*, Gregory M. Bounds and John A. Woods make an important point on the difference between *awards* and *recognition*. They assert that employees tend to treat awards as goals, as the purpose for doing their jobs. If they receive an award, they may not feel any need to continue their efforts. On the other hand, according to Bounds and Woods, recognition—if given appropriately—is not a goal for employees, but an affirmation that they're doing a good job and encouragement to continue and to do even better.

So, what can you do? Here are some suggestions from Donna Deeprose's book, *The Team Coach*.

- Arrange for a thank-you visit or letter from the president or vice president of your organization.
- Send thank-you letters or memos, written by hand or sent by e-mail.
- Send letters to the families of your team members to express appreciation for what the team has done and to explain the importance of the efforts. This is especially appropriate when the work has involved overtime. Also thank the families for being understanding and supportive.

- Put an article about your team and its accomplishments in the organization's newsletter.
- Arrange for your team to present a report on its efforts and accomplishments to top management.
- Take the team out to lunch.

These are just a few of many possibilities. How you choose to recognize your employees depends on three factors.

How you show recognition depends, of course, on *the accomplishment* you're recognizing. It's nice to be enthusiastic, but it could seem excessive, maybe even embarrassingly so, if you took the team out to lunch every other day to celebrate something.

Recognition also depends on *the size and structure of the organization.* If you don't have a newsletter, for example, you might post an announcement about your team and its accomplishments on bulletin boards around the organization or use e-mail to notify all employees.

Finally, recognition depends in large part, as we've stressed throughout this book, on the culture of your workplace, on *what your employees value.* For example, if you know that your people generally dislike the president, you'd be wise not to ask for a letter from the top as a sign of recognition.

Coaching by Example

I'll keep this section brief. Practice what you preach. Be a model employee, team member, and coach if you expect your employees to develop as employees and team members and to be better coaches.

Yeah, it's difficult. You may not get along with some of the other managers. You may feel pressured sometimes to do less than your best. You may not always be positive or appreciate the people around you. You may feel overwhelmed or

Smart Managing

A Good Example

Oliver Goldsmith once noted, "People seldom improve when they have no other model but themselves to copy."

Provide that model—and make sure it's exemplary.

frustrated or even angry. You may be distracted or absorbed in another matter, so you aren't really listening. That's natural—you're only human.

Now, imagine that you're surrounded by other humans, each of them picking up signs from you, each ready to follow your lead. That's natural, too. But is that what you want?

Manager's Checklist for Chapter 9

❑ Coaching is the most effective means of empowering a team and helping its members develop.

❑ As coach, you have two goals: to improve work performance and to help your players develop teamwork and leadership.

❑ Coaching is a performance skill; you master it only through practice and feedback.

❑ Every member of the team has a responsibility for coaching his or her teammates as appropriate—and for coaching you, their manager and head coach.

❑ Perhaps the most important yet often neglected part of the coaching process is to provide recognition for the players, formally and informally. Be creative in seeking out opportunities.

❑ The best way to help your people develop as employees, team members, and coaches is by setting a great example.

Coping with Conflicts and Changes

As manager and team leader, you've got to cope with conflicts and changes. In this chapter I'll recommend ways to do so more effectively—and make your job easier.

Resolving Conflicts

Although conflict is normal with teamwork, when it gets out of control, it can wreck teamwork and cut into productivity. The only way to handle conflict is to deal with it directly.

Trust your teammates to work out their differences—and help them develop skills for resolving their conflicts. The method that I recommend for teams is *direct dealing*.

Direct dealing is an approach to problem solving that emphasizes person-to-person communication. As such, it fits in with other skills your team members will be learning to apply. Direct dealing encourages team members to work out their problems without going to management, thus avoiding complications, saving time and energy, and minimizing possible distortions of issues. By following a set of guidelines, both managers and team members can learn how to solve their problems in an open, evenhanded way, without third parties or unnecessary refereeing.

Both team members and managers must model direct dealing behaviors and help to create a climate that supports direct dealing. If team members see managers as approachable and understanding of conflicts, they're far more likely to deal directly.

In creating the climate for direct dealing, you must:
- Learn what direct dealing is.
- Be able to provide examples of direct dealing.
- Support and encourage the use of direct dealing by team members.
- Seek opportunities to demonstrate direct dealing.
- Train new team members in direct dealing.
- Make direct dealing a part of everyday work.

Direct Dealing

The principles of direct dealing are simple, but they get lost in many organizations. Whoever is involved in a confrontation is responsible for trying to resolve the conflict, through one-on-one dialogue, using the techniques outlined here. If that doesn't work, the parties can request assistance from a third party, who then should be empowered to settle the conflict. It's simple and it keeps conflicts from spreading.

The Process of Direct Dealing

If you're a member of a team, at some time you're probably going to need to confront a teammate about a problem. This puts you in a difficult situation and raises the potential for conflict. To minimize conflict, follow these steps when confronting a team member. Of course, if you resolve the problem, there's no need to take any further steps.

Step 1: Tell your teammate that you've got a problem with something he or she has done. Suggest that the problem may be a misunderstanding and express your interest in listening to him or her. Listen actively without offering any counterarguments.

Step 2: Plan a meeting with the teammate. Review the problem and explore it in more detail. Use the Direct Dealing Guidelines.

Step 3: Confront the teammate with the problem. Suggest that he or she may need some help in dealing with the problem.
Step 4: Bring the problem up to the whole team and ask for input from all teammates.
Step 5: As a team, refer the problem and the problem teammate to management.

The Direct Dealing Guidelines

The purpose of these guidelines is to provide a structure for direct dealing encounters. The guidelines are intentionally short and simple to encourage their use. Read the guidelines and put a check next to items that are useful tactics for your particular style.

1. **State the problem in specific, behavioral terms.**
   * Identify the problem using examples.
   * Describe the consequences of the problem.
   * Avoid generalities like "always" or "never."
   * Deal with facts, not opinions.
   * Avoid personal attacks.
   * Use "We" rather than "You" when describing the problem.
2. **Explain the impact of the problem.**
   * Show how the problem affects the team's operation.
   * Describe costs, delays, and quality problems.
   * Identify both human and business impacts.
   * Review the history of the problem and how it arose.
   * Describe efforts taken to deal with the problem.
3. **Listen to the other person's point of view.**
   * Ask for the other person's ideas and feelings before expressing your own.
   * Determine whether the other person perceives the problem as you do.
   * Probe for additional concerns by asking, "What else can you tell me?"
   * Seek out resistance to change and identify the source.
   * Restate concerns and express your willingness to establish common ground.

4. **Establish common ground.**
   - Test for common ground by proposing an initial solution.
   - Show flexibility in planning for change.
5. **Express an interest in the other's ideas, even if they don't eliminate the problem.**
   - Identify mutual benefits for any idea.
   - Brainstorm alternative actions.
   - Establish a follow-up plan.

Barriers to Direct Dealing

Here are some personal and organizational barriers to direct dealing and tactics for overcoming those barriers.

Barrier: Fear of Confrontation. Most of us have it deeply ingrained in our personality, from kindergarten on, to avoid confrontation and seek harmony.
Tactics:
   - Address the problem when it's still minor.
   - Practice with your teammates.
   - Invite the other party to your team meeting.
   - Select a nonthreatening time and place.

Barrier: Lack of Support. Without a culture that supports taking the lead in confronting tough situations, few people want to risk their jobs and personal comfort.
Tactics:
   - Have management visibly support the process.
   - Discuss the process during team meetings.
   - Have a written policy statement and guidelines.
   - Provide training in the policy.

Barrier: Different Power Levels. When dealing with people at upper levels, the threat of reprisal is on everyone's mind.
Tactics:
   - Train managers to deal with assertive employees.
   - Celebrate examples of successful changes brought about through direct dealing.
   - Have a policy that protects employees.
   - Train employees and managers together.

Barrier: Lack of Information. When challenging a process or system, it's important to have the facts on your side. Sometimes data are difficult or impossible to obtain when teams are already under pressure to do their regular work.

Tactics:

- Keep channels to administration open to teams.
- Provide on-line systems availability.
- Train employees in basic business processes.
- Provide paid time to research projects.

Barrier: Concern for Consequences. It's tough to risk angering a co-worker who can retaliate.

Tactics:

- Have "open" team meetings where "customers" and "suppliers" are invited to air gripes.
- Reinforce the importance of staying open to all team members.

Barrier: Lack of Skills. Confronting difficult situations, diffusing emotions, and arriving at consensus require good negotiating skills.

Tactics:

- Train, train, train.
- Provide reinforcement and refresher courses.
- Practice within the team.
- Get coaching from team leaders or facilitator.

Barrier: Lack of a Formal Process. Without a process for direct dealing, people must fend for themselves.

Tactics:

- Create, publish, and discuss the policy.
- Have senior people use and support the policy.
- Provide training on the process and steps for using it.

The Role of a "Third Party"

Sometimes one-on-one doesn't work. When this happens, employees have the option of kicking the problem "upstairs" to management, where it will be settled. But before a conflict reaches that point, it may be a good idea for the team or a team member trusted by either party to intercede as a third party. The role of this third party is not to force a decision, but to apply facilitation skills to free up entrenched positions.

Warning! There's always a risk that a third party may become part of the problem. To handle the role properly, follow these guidelines:

- Stay cool, stay neutral.
- Continue to get back to the facts.
- Avoid trying to resolve the conflict yourself. Act as a coach, mentor, or counselor to both parties to help them resolve their problem.
- Withdraw from the situation as soon as the two parties seem able to move forward with solutions on their own.
- Beware of slipping into the role of rescuer or pal.

Do-It-Yourself Skill Practice

The do-it-yourself skill practice is not a role-play. It's more like a planning session to help you put your thoughts in order and plan a direct dealing encounter.

Use the Planning Guide (Figure 10-1) to help think through the issues you want to discuss. After you complete it, work with a team member and practice holding a meeting using the Direct Dealing Guidelines. Have a third person observe, using the Observer Feedback Form (Figure 10-2, on page 157).

A Tool for Dealing with Conflicts

Direct dealing provides a great structured method for resolving conflicts. It can be even more effective if your employees know about reflecting—a general technique that's valuable in two-way communication. (It's not just for your employees. You can easily learn to use it naturally in almost any face-to-face with your employees.)

What is reflecting? It's a mirroring technique. You simply reflect back the concerns expressed by the other person, showing you're listening and value him or her and the needs voiced in those concerns.

This technique enables you to get more information from

Planning Guide

Name of person

What is the problem?

Problem Details

• What and where?

• Costs or consequences?

• How long a problem?

Suggested Actions

Background information (Other direct dealing attempts? How does the other person feel about the problem?)

How will you break the ice?

Figure 10-1. Planning guide

people without asking a lot of questions and making them feel more uncomfortable, even defensive. You can get that person to talk more, while you listen more effectively, keeping your opinions and biases from intruding into the conversation.

In dealing with differences, doing what usually comes most naturally—pushing your point of view—only builds resistance and further conflict. Doing the unexpected—listening and asking for more, not less, from the other person—opens the communication channels.

Observer Feedback Form

Circle the number that best represents your thoughts on each question. To what extent did the Direct Dealing Initiator:	Not much	To some extent	A lot
1. State the problem in specific behavioral terms? Example:	1 2 3		4 5
2. Explain the impact of the problem? Example:	1 2 3		4 5
3. Listen to the other person's point of view? Example:	1 2 3		4 5
4. Establish common ground? Example:	1 2 3		4 5

Figure 10-2. Observer feedback form

Guidelines for Reflecting

Use these guidelines to help reduce conflict and build trust.

1. Be prepared.
- Know what to expect by talking to others.
- Have a thorough understanding of likely objections.
- Consider what could go wrong.
- Get your facts and figures in advance.
- Have a back-up position.

2. State the problem.
- State your concerns.
- Explain why you need support or cooperation.
- Say what you want to accomplish.

3. Explore concerns and objections.
- Ask open questions.
- Avoid responding too soon.
- Take notes.
- Ask for implications.
- Use positive body language.

4. Support concerns.
- Don't defend your position.
- Acknowledge the other's concerns.
- Agree that the concerns are valid.
- Empathize: "I understand how you feel."

5. Respond actively.
- Indicate you're willing to act on those concerns.
- Suggest compromises.

6. Get closure and establish follow-up.
- Check to make sure the other person agrees on any decisions.
- Summarize the next steps to take.
- Thank the person.
- Follow up on any decisions.

Advantages of Direct Dealing to Resolve Conflicts

Direct dealing empowers team members and helps them make informed decisions through individual responsibility, personal growth, and access to decision-making tools. This method is often hard at first, but it can become a part of the way a team handles all of its conflicts.

The Direct Dealing Guidelines help establish a common language that every team member can understand and use without fear of conflict and misunderstanding. But it's not enough to train your team members to use direct dealing. In order to foster direct dealing, management must create a climate that facilitates one-on-

Key Term **Reflecting** A technique for more effective communication, particularly in situations of potential conflict. You reflect by mirroring the concerns expressed by the other person, to show that you understand and appreciate those concerns and value that person.

one problem solving. Above all, managers should be very wary about getting involved in conflicts. Becoming a third party in one-on-one conflict resolution is a role that managers should accept only when the two parties have failed to resolve their conflict and request assistance.

Reducing Conflicts

Direct dealing is a great way to resolve conflicts. But the best way to manage conflicts is to understand what causes them and how to make them less likely. Team members should be aware of the sources of conflict and understand how their own behavior can either minimize or aggravate conflict.

Sources of Conflict

We can't hope to cover all the possible sources of conflicts in this chapter. Let's focus on those most likely to occur as you implement teams, and show how you should move from intervention strategies to direct dealing.

A common way to discuss team development is in terms of four stages—forming, storming, norming, and performing. As a team progresses through its developmental stages, the sources of conflict tend to be different, so it's generally more effective to use different strategies for dealing with conflicts.

Forming: The stage of transition from individuals to team members. People try to be polite, to suppress any conflict. Many feel there's no room for conflict because they're a team and teams should stress unity.

Conflict Resolution Strategies: The leader intervenes

> **CAUTION!**
>
> ### Body Talk
> What's your body saying about you? Are you sending signals that you're defensive? suspicious? confused? angry? unlikely to compromise? If your body is expressing negative feelings, it may not matter much what you put into your words.
>
> You don't need to read a book on body language—although it's a good idea. You can simply pay more attention to the body language you see all around you, in movies, and on TV. Then use what you learn to make sure your body isn't sabotaging your communication.

or conflicting individuals avoid each other. It's usually not appropriate to expect team members to use direct dealing.

Storming: The stage of turbulence, of dissonance. There are personal conflicts and conflicts over work, resources, team goals, and rewards. Expectations are less idealistic, causing a sense of disillusionment, and the slow pace of development frustrates many members.

Conflict Resolution Strategies: The team should practice conflict resolution tactics during meetings and sometimes one on one. There are lots of opportunities for direct dealing.

Norming: This is the stage of acceptance, of reconciling differences. Conflict usually occurs under special situations, such as accidents, work-related problems, job stress, overtime, workload, or turnover.

Conflict Resolution Strategies: The use of conflict resolution tactics such as direct dealing improves.

Performing: This is the stage of accomplishment. Team members have learned how to work well together. Conflict comes when the team interacts with other teams or outsiders.

Conflict Resolution Strategies: Individuals solve their own conflicts, with little need for team support or intervention from the leader.

How People Handle Conflict

Of course, you can't try to understand conflicts simply in terms of stages in a team's development. You don't need a Ph.D. in psychology to know that individuals deal with differences in various ways. But it may help you to understand reactions to conflict in terms of four styles:

- Avoiding
- Accommodating
- Confronting
- Collaborating

The following behavioral descriptions should help you recognize these four types of reactions as they appear in group situations, so you can work with them appropriately. Perhaps the best way is to share the following section with your team members. They can then better understand themselves and try to develop more effective ways to approach conflict.

Avoiding

General behavior: You wait the problem out. (These things usually get resolved.)

The following statements express an Avoiding style:

1. The best behavior in problem-solving meetings is to mind your own business.
2. Sticking to your job is better than trying to change things.
3. No one is interested in my opinion.
4. By keeping to myself, I stay out of trouble.
5. I avoid people with strong convictions.
6. The best way to avoid rejection is to avoid making suggestions.
7. I'm more productive working alone than on a team.
8. The supervisor should resolve disagreements.
9. I try to do my work and not worry about what others do.
10. When people work together, problems are inevitable.
11. Trying new things is risky and could get you into trouble.
12. If we could cut out all these meetings, we would get a lot more done here.

Advantages of Avoiding:
- People view you as cautious and hard working.
- You're recognized more for your work skills than for your teamwork.
- You're known for your no-nonsense style.
- You don't get involved in political wrangling.

Disadvantages of Avoiding:
- You seldom take the opportunity to provide input.
- You're seen as uncommitted.
- People may not trust you.
- You tend to be frustrated working in a team environment.

Bottom Line: By avoiding conflict, you withdraw as a contributing team member. You may also fail to use direct dealing techniques, allowing others to have their way rather than risk confrontation. In difficult situations, you prefer to work alone.

Accommodating

General behavior: You seek support for your point of view, but go with the majority in the end.

The following statements express an Accommodating style:

1. I'm ready to let others have their way if it doesn't inconvenience me.
2. In unfamiliar situations I let others with more confidence take the lead.
3. In the end, getting along is more important than getting your ideas across.
4. My idea of a good work environment is one where everybody gets along and there's no conflict.
5. It's more important to be liked than to have people do things your way.
6. Issues at work are just not worth arguing about.
7. The best policy at work is to try to do what you're told by your superiors.
8. I'm not sure my ideas are the best, so I don't push them.
9. At work, it's smartest to keep your ideas to yourself.
10. The secret of success is knowing when to quit.

Advantages of Accommodating:

- People like you.
- You're not viewed as a threat or troublemaker.
- You're a good team member.
- You do well socially.

Disadvantages of Accommodating:

- Go-getters don't respect you.
- People view you as a yes-person.
- You seldom provide much input.
- You suffer stress from your lack of assertiveness.

Bottom Line: If you're too accommodating, you risk giving in on matters where you should hold your ground. Though you may be seen as easygoing and pleasant, a "good team player," you may contribute less than you should to the team's alternatives by going along with the majority.

Confronting

General behavior: You express your point of view forcefully and directly.

The following statements express a Confronting style:

1. I'm not afraid to state my point forcefully if I feel strongly about it.
2. For people to pay attention, you've got to assert yourself.
3. I'm known as a person who likes to win.
4. To me, compromising means losing something I want.
5. Compromises usually ruin good ideas.
6. If people would listen to what I say, they'd realize I'm usually right.
7. Among all my co-workers, I usually have the best ideas.
8. It's important to fight hard to get your way.
9. The secret of success is never backing down.
10. Compromise can be a sign of weakness.

Advantages of Confronting:
- You often take charge in chaotic situations.
- You can be seen as a leader.
- Your ideas get an airing.
- Others must take you into consideration.

Disadvantages of Confronting:
- People view you as pushy.
- You may listen too little.
- You create as much conflict as you resolve.
- You alienate allies.

Bottom Line: You try to ensure that your ideas are adopted and followed, and you assert yourself during meetings and in most work-related situations. This tends to intimidate your team-mates. You feel that the only way to contribute is to forcefully push your ideas and display your talent. That approach, unfortunately, undermines team efforts by reducing the potential contributions of the other team members.

Collaborating

General behavior: You take the lead in trying to get consensus on a solution to the problem.

The following statements express a Collaborating style:

1. Dealing with conflict is a natural part of achieving goals.
2. I learn something new when I listen to others' ideas.
3. The best ideas come when everybody contributes.
4. Never go ahead with a decision unless everyone can live with it.
5. Teams make better decisions than individuals alone.
6. Healthy conflict can often produce better ideas.
7. I'm responsible for presenting my point of view.
8. Two heads are better than one.
9. Sometimes the best ideas come from the least expected sources.
10. We should listen more than we speak.
11. I'd rather work through problems as a team than by myself.
12. I insist on addressing everyone's concerns before taking action.

Advantages of Collaborating:

- People consider you a leader.
- You help develop your teammates.
- You force important issues to the surface.
- You can build strong alliances.

Disadvantages of Collaborating:

- It may seem to others like you're wasting time.
- People may think you're a phony, management's pet, a wimp.
- You sometimes lose your own thoughts when concentrating on others.
- You function poorly in an autocratic organization.

Bottom Line: It's important to you to make sure all team members participate and work together. You especially like decisions by consensus. You tend to get actively involved, quite often as a facilitator, helping your teammates step forward with new ideas and take risks.

Coping with Changes

Change is a particular source of conflict. Each of us has problems accepting change and adapting to it. It's worse in a group, because our individual differences tend to multiply the problems caused by changes.

But there's a critical difference between conflict and change. Though we may try to resolve conflict and minimize the effects, we must welcome change as inevitable and necessary, then adapt to the effects.

Why People Resist Change

People resist change for a variety of reasons, some of which are perfectly sound. In fact, resistance to change is natural. It might even represent a very appropriate survival response. We know, for instance, that too much change, even too much positive change—e.g., a new job, new home, new spouse, children—can produce physiological symptoms similar to those induced by painful stress.

Here are some of the causes of resistance that you may encounter as you implement teams.

Loss of control: How people greet change depends on whether they feel they can control the change or not. Is the change something that's being done to us or something we're doing together?

Too much uncertainty: Management fails to convey a sense that the change is right and proper and that they have confidence in it. Management tells the employees, "You first, I'll follow."

Surprise: The managers ponder the change in private and then, when it's all ready, they spring it on the staff. The first reaction—shock—often undermines acceptance and adaptation.

Too much change: Too often managers seem to feel that if they have to change something, they might as well change everything all at once. That approach removes familiar anchors that might help employees better accept the changes.

Doubts about the past: Change that forces people to admit that they've been doing things wrong all along causes resentment and resistance.

Fear of failure: People resist change when they fear they won't be able to cope with the new demands.

Ripple effects: Major changes produce wholly unanticipated effects on people's lives. While employees may be willing to go along with the business aspects of the change, ripple effects can cause them to resist.

Two Basic Rules of Life

Smart Managing

1. Change is inevitable.
2. Everyone resists change.
    Smart managers remind everybody about the first rule—and never forget the second rule. The more you can get people to accept the first rule, the less you have to worry about the second.

More work: Changes cause more work, because the change often demands stable performance on the current job and extra effort to incorporate the changes. This results in long hours and burnout.

Past resentments: Employees may resist change because they harbor resentments against the organization or the managers from earlier changes.

Real risks: When change means that employees may suffer in status, have fewer opportunities, be required to move, or lose their jobs, they'll quite naturally resist.

Managing Changes More Effectively

As a manager, you can do things differently to reduce resistance to change, to make it easier for your employees to accept and adapt. How well do you manage changes? Rate yourself according to the following statements—from the perspective of your employees. If you're brave, you may even want to make copies so your employees can evaluate how you manage changes.

1. He/She clearly communicated to my co-workers and me the nature of the changes.
2. He/She helped all employees affected understand the changes and the reasons for them.
3. In planning and making the changes, he/she considered the benefits (opportunities) and barriers (problems) for our department.
4. He/She clearly identified the differences between how we were doing things then and how we would do things as a result of the changes.
5. He/She involved all those who would be affected by the change in the decision/planning process.
6. When communicating about the changes, he/she discussed new roles, responsibilities, and relationships.
7. He/She heard and addressed the concerns of the employees.
8. He/She checked to make sure we all understood what was communicated.
9. He/She made sure that we all received the knowledge/ skills training we would need for our tasks and responsibilities.
10. He/She made sure the necessary resources and assistance were provided to those responsible for making the changes.

Minimizing the Ripples

You can minimize the ripple effect with the proper approach to planning. This is one time when it pays to disregard the advice in that old song, "Accentuate the positive, eliminate the negative."

Try to always consider every change from every perspective. Think creatively. Insist on asking, "What if ...?" as many times as possible. Play the pessimist and generate worst-case scenarios.

You can't get away from the ripple effect. But when you know where the ripples are likely to go, you can anticipate them and reduce the negative effects on your employees.

11. He/She developed a method to monitor the impact and effectiveness of the change.
12. The change was implemented successfully.

So, how did you rate on those 12 statements? If you didn't do as well as you expected, you may want to put a copy of that list of statements on your office wall, to keep in mind.

What else can you do to manage changes more effectively? Here are some tactics:

- Allow room for your employees to participate in planning for anticipated changes. Get them involved, survey them, ask for input.
- Stay flexible on the details. Let your employees organize themselves to adapt to the changes. Provide guidelines, but allow for individual adjustments.
- Provide a vision of the changes coming. Let your employees see the big picture and try to show how the final goals will be beneficial to all.
- Share information about changes before they affect your employees.
- Divide big changes into little changes. Do one thing at a time, in proper sequence.
- Plan ahead for changes. Allow time for your employees to digest the proposed changes and get used to them. Then, and only then, move ahead with the changes.
- Get in front of the change initiative with your management team and demonstrate the value of the changes. If the changes demand new performance standards, be specific about them. Don't wait for mistakes.

Easy Change

Smart Managing "People don't resist change; they resist being changed." You may not agree with this assertion by Peter R. Scholtes, author of *The Team Handbook*. But you can certainly believe that the more your employees feel that changes are being imposed on them, the more they're likely to resist. A smart manager tries to make change easier for everyone in the organization.

- Reinforce and praise. Coach for the changes and let your employees know they can succeed in the change process.
- Find and reward early successes, pioneers in the change efforts. Identify models and celebrate successes.
- Find ways to reward your employees for the extra effort and time required by the changes. Look for opportunities to praise, party, and pay.
- Deal honestly and equitably with those negatively affected by the changes. Help them to adjust; don't just ignore them until they leave. How you treat them sends messages about what your other employees can expect.
- Remember: people won't resist changes from which they expect to benefit. Help your employees answer that basic question—"What's in it for me?"

Manager's Checklist for Chapter 10

❑ Trust your team members to work out their differences. Help them develop skills for resolving their conflicts. Two simple, effective methods for resolving conflict are direct dealing and reflecting.

❑ If you're called into a conflict as a "third party," know what role you should play and avoid other involvement by following basic guidelines.

❑ To avoid conflict when initiating organization-wide changes, plan the changes as if they were a large-scale business venture. Evaluate the market, assess the risk, dedicate the resources, and initiate an aggressive program of marketing.

❑ Understand the four ways of reacting to conflict—avoiding, accommodating, confronting, and collaborating—and learn how to work with them appropriately.

❑ Anticipate problems accepting change and adapting to it. Help your employees welcome change as inevitable and necessary—and work to minimize the problems.

Applied Empowerment

For many, empowerment sometimes seems like organizational castor oil. Like that old panacea, we think it's good for us although (because?) it tastes terrible. We take it when we're sluggish and need to feel better fast. It treats the symptoms but does nothing for the causes. Holding our noses, we swallow it all at once, endure the outcome, recover, and then try to forget about it until the next time we need it.

When management deals with empowerment this way, it produces results remarkably similar to those produced by castor oil. Then the rest of us, from consultants to partially empowered teams, have to deal with what remains.

But perhaps we should be more generous. After all, empowering teams involves complex processes. No manager wants to admit to having a problem with it, but almost all of them find it difficult.

Problems with Empowerment

Here are some examples of problems with implementing empowerment programs.

Case #1: A large healthcare organization decided to create self-directed teams, but involve the physicians.

The result: the docs didn't show up for case management reviews, decisions were postponed, patients waited for service, and the team members were so discouraged that they disbanded.

Case #2: The president of a bank holding company fell in love with the idea of empowerment and told his training manager to get on with it. Six months later teams had been formed, training had begun, and the roles of supervisors were being challenged. The problem? The vice presidents weren't brought into the picture and resisted changes proposed from the bottom up. They stalled the effort with questions and suspicion, caused the teams to wonder about whether the effort had support, and created problems.

Case #3: A start-up manufacturing plant made major time and financial commitments to forming teams, training the teams, and several rounds of management training. The missing link: they failed to measure team progress. Instead of setting goals for their teams and holding them responsible for achieving those goals, the managers closed their eyes, crossed their fingers, and hoped that everything would work out. It didn't—and a senior manager from headquarters wound up intervening to make sure the project was under control.

Case #4: A manufacturer went from six to three layers in its international organization with an eye to profits and speedier re-engineered systems. They initiated a well-defined, top-down approach to creating high-performance teams. But they didn't conduct an assessment of current practices among all the sites. If they had, they would have discovered that some locations were already very advanced in their team programs and others were years behind. Instead of taking a top-down, "Do as you're told!" approach, they could have initiated surgical efforts costing less and paying off quicker.

Case #5: A fast-growing, customer-oriented restaurant chain decided to implement team training on the cheap. They were accustomed to mass hiring and such high turnover that it was a point of honor with them to spend less than the low industry average on training per hire. They condensed the training to four two-hour sessions, baffling employees as to what they wanted, while raising unrealistic expectations about what they could and couldn't do without permission from management.

Planning Too Little and Expecting Too Much

How are these five cases similar? In each, the managers wanted to do the right thing. They understood that empowerment requires both commitment and resources. Their errors were not strategic, but tactical. They failed to think through the process, consider potential problems, ask a few hard questions, and, in short, spend the time to consider their goals and how they would be received and interpreted by employees.

Empowerment Delegating responsibility and authority to employees to make decisions and take action. But that's only part of the working definition. Employees also need preparation to assume and exercise their new power.

It's easy to take shots at managers for expecting their teams to do too much, too soon, without adequate resources and training. But it's only natural for them to have excessively high expectations. They expect too much when they empower teams because, in many cases, they learned that lesson from above: their own managers have expected too much when empowering them. They just don't know or don't remember how to develop and nurture people to work independently and creatively. In short, the management model for delega-

Empowerment and Results

A middle manager in a paper plant expressed it this way: "When I thought about empowerment, I thought about the *results*, not the *process*. For me it was a done deal the moment I announced it. I saw teams making all kinds of decisions on their own, budgeting, hiring, taking responsibility for quality, team meetings—the whole thing. I really never thought about the details. I guess I was just too concerned with seeing it done."

The moral of the story: optimism and high expectations can hurt teams worse than negativity.

tion has been the bucket brigade rather than the hourglass.

If it's hard to get managers to take a sustained and detailed look at the actual process of empowerment, it's nearly impossible to involve them in team activities in which new tasks are considered, boundaries bashed, or roles rewritten. Sitting through team meetings can be boring and a real act of will power when there are other more pressing matters. This kind of commitment takes time—and that's something managers don't seem to be able to afford.

For many, the intuitively correct solution is to go back to the cultural drawing board. With rulers, markers, charts, and tape, we'd like the opportunity to work with executive groups, boards, and management teams and re-engineer—not processes, but visions, goals, missions, and values. We want to tinker with the senior team until everything is perfect. We want to involve the workers through focus groups in which we can enlist their spirits, plunge our hands into the history books of their experience, and come away with confirmation of our plan. We want to roll this plan out with fanfare, free lunches, a video, and the chair giving promises and assurances. We want our plan to be one in which everyone wins, each has a role to play, the rules are unambiguous, resources are sufficient, goals are clear, and we achieve the results we expect.

But, welcome to the '90s! Life's not like that anymore. I haven't facilitated a vision workshop in four years that's lasted longer than a day. I can't get managers to sit through training sessions longer than two days. I've been forced to employ every gram of persuasion I have to get work teams to drop their mouses or hammers and sit down and meet once a week. When I say that empowerment takes years, eyes cloud over and someone from Cincinnati pipes up that their team was totally empowered in a week, everyone was very happy, and what's the big deal?

Perhaps we need a new paradigm for the kind of intervention that makes empowerment work in unfavorable or indifferent environments. The old models of realigning and repositioning organizational cultures through a kind of long-term therapy are out the window for now. What we need is a simpler approach.

A Simpler Approach

In a robotics lab somewhere in the cavernous warren of labs that make up MIT, there squats an ungainly body of nuts and bolts that students have programmed to wander around the lab at night picking up empty soda cans and depositing them in the recycling bin. At the end of its rounds, this R2D2 predecessor parks itself in the corner and shuts down.

That's all rather sophomoric—with one exceptional result. From this random picking-up activity, MIT thinkers have abstracted a set of principles that seem to govern the error-free, yet simple programming that propels this recycling robot.

Without a central program, human intervention, or constant tweaking of its program, the robot performs flawlessly. From this experience has emerged a set of principles:

1. Do the basics first.
2. Learn to do things flawlessly.
3. Add new tasks only as previous tasks are mastered.
4. Make the new tasks work as flawlessly as the basic ones.
5. Repeat, ad infinitum.

A nice set of principles. Also a good outline for this chapter—and any other aspiring efforts on how to do more with less, do it without tight controls, and instill the principles of outstanding and consistent performance at all levels. In short, successful empowerment.

To play this metaphor out, let's substitute *teams* for *machine, tasks* for *cans,* and *workplace* for *lab.* For the *lack of human intervention or a central program,* let's just say *limited management involvement* and leave it at that. Let's also accept *flawlessly,* since we're stuck with high standards whether we like it or not. To fall short of that goal might mean we'll get disassembled in the morning and re-engineered in the afternoon. In that respect as well, teams and machines face a common fate: obsolescence.

Now, let's apply those five principles to empowerment.

Do the Basics First

Begin with a definition and a set of goals. Have a plan that you clearly articulate and communicate to the teams involved.

It's amazing how many organizations simply skip this step or leave it to training and human resources to take care of. Try as they might, they can't handle those managerial responsibilities.

Empowerment requires a specific, operational definition that fits the company culture and language. Here's the definition that I use, since it encompasses a lot while showing how all aspects of work interrelate:

> *Empowerment is a process*
> *for helping the **right people***
> *at the **right levels***
> *make the **right decisions***
> *for the **right reasons.***

This definition asks a lot. But it also provides a lot. In working with managers who honestly seek empowerment and the benefits that come with it, we spend time analyzing that definition. The questions that emerge often give them pause. They quickly realize that they haven't considered some of the consequences of empowerment or done their homework.

The following questions, posed by our definition, need to be asked and answered to the satisfaction of all involved:

Right People
- "Who should we target to begin an empowerment effort?"
- "Is there some way to determine which group is best suited for empowerment and self-direction?"
- "Can anyone be empowered? Or are we stuck with what we hired?"
- "How do we deal with people who don't seem to want to take responsibility?"

Right Levels
- "What kinds of decisions should people be making on their own? What are the boundaries?"
- "How much authority can you push down the line? And how quickly can you do it?"

- "How do you track the *effectiveness* of a delegation? How do you make sure things are getting done?"
- "Who does the team report to? What are the differences between managing team performance and managing individual performance?"
- "How do you deal with people's expectations to be individually recognized and promoted? Is responsibility and authority an adequate substitute for a management job title?"

Right Decisions

- "What are the right decisions?"
- "What are the boundaries of decision making? What should people be tackling now, three months from now, six months from now, next year?"
- "What is management's role in decision making? If we say 'Be empowered,' does that mean 'Hands off' for managers?"
- "What if we see people making wrong or somewhat wrong decisions? Can we intervene without sinking the team?"

Right Reasons

- "How much knowledge and education does the team really need to make good decisions?"
- "What's our investment in training going to be? Can we really afford it?"
- "Do we actually intend to invest more power and decision making in our people?"
- "Is this a long-term business strategy and are we willing to make a commitment to not jerking people around?"

By asking and answering these questions, managers can begin to grasp the scope of their empowerment strategy. They can avoid a lengthy and somewhat redundant socio-technical analysis yet deal with the key issues and make some of the important preliminary decisions.

It's impossible to get it right the first time, but it's inexcusable to avoid asking the right questions. I can't provide all the answers to these questions. But I can offer a few tips to make your empowerment process work more effectively.

Learn to Do Things Flawlessly

Treat every empowerment delegation as though it's your last. Don't move on until you've got it down cold.

There's no mystery in doing the basics: housekeeping, vacation planning, shift coverage, even phone coverage. What's hard is the human side of engineering tasks, including rotating jobs, maintaining standards, taking responsibility for them, and transferring them to others. If you allow a team to move on to the next task before it's mastered the present one, you're condoning mediocre performance and lowering standards.

You cannot assume that abilities will necessarily apply naturally to new tasks. Employees who can balance a checkbook, mow the lawn when the grass gets high, or select a contractor to put on a new roof can't necessarily be expected to coordinate a team budget, plan preventive maintenance, deal with vendors and suppliers, or select new team members. Instead, those tasks are new, in an unfamiliar environment. Of course, some skills and experiences do transfer, some personal and some related to the work. But if you don't make plans to shift these skills from the personal realm to the organizational, don't expect the transfer to happen naturally.

> ### Getting the Questions Asked
> **Smart Managing**
>
> Are any of your fellow managers skeptical about empowerment? Are there any "professional cynics" in your organization?
>
> This is where you can tap those usually less respected and valued talents. Just invite those managers to come up with questions. They can probably do so with the greatest of ease. And then everyone can address them, helping to reduce such cynicism and improving chances for success.

Ensuring flawless performance—or performance of any sort—isn't easy. It takes time, planning, and a measurement system that tracks each step of the learning process. The key to empowerment is basically in making sure the transfer of a task is successful.

A solution to this problem of ensuring consistent performance is being tried at a certain financial company. A team

leader there has devised a system to ensure that each department responsible for pushing empowerment into the ranks has
a written plan in place. It's neither complicated nor even particularly demanding, but it requires each manager to think
through the tasks that will be delegated, answer how that task
is currently handled, and set a goal for when it will be assumed by the team. That way, each team has a plan for empowerment, in writing.

> **⚠ CAUTION!**
>
> ## It's Just Like...
> Three little words can undermine your teams—"It's just like ...." Sure, we all naturally learn new things in terms of what we already know, but we can't assume any guarantee of easy success with any new task or responsibility simply because we assume "it's just like ..."—because maybe it isn't.

The plan consists of a matrix (Figure 11-1) that lists the kind of empow-erment actions that teams will be asked to assume during the next few years. A generic list is provided that helps managers think through a broad range of actions, but managers and staff must work together to customize that list to build the final docu-ment.

Once the list is built, the managers need to ask two questions:

1. Who is *currently* responsible for this task?
2. What will be the team's role when the empowerment dele-gation is complete?

To simplify things, colors are used to indicate current and future authority for each task:

Red— management is responsible for the task.

Yellow—the team will have input into the task.

Blue—the team and management will jointly take responsi-bility for the task.

Green—the task is in the hands of the team, without man-agement involvement.

In addition to indicating current responsibility and target responsibility, colors are used to provide guidelines for the gradual handoff of responsibilities over the period of the dele-

	Present	Goal	0-3 Months	3-6 Months	6-9 Months	9-12 Months	12-18 Months	18-24 Months	2-3 Years
Firing	Red	Red							
Hiring	Red	Green			Yellow	Blue	Green		
Meetings	Red	Green	Yellow	Blue	Green				
Staffing/ Work Schedules	Yellow	Green				Yellow		Blue	Green
Overtime Scheduling	Red	Blue		Yellow		Blue			

Figure 11-1. Empowerment schedule

gation, from a few months to beyond a year. The colors provide a quick picture of who's doing what, and managers and team members are able to build a plan for every task over a specified time period.

A "succession plan" like this ensures a smoother transition of authority from manager to team. Delay new tasks until the team has demonstrated competence in a current task.

Add New Tasks Only as Previous Tasks Are Mastered

"Mastery," "consistency," "control," "uniformity," and "direction" are words seldom associated with either self-managing teams or empowerment. But performance management is critical if we want to make sure we'll meet our empowerment goals and that the process will move along at a steady pace.

In our experience, a sure symptom of a weak performance management process is when a team's ambitions outpace its abilities. When teams start complaining because management doesn't want them hiring, firing, budgeting, or doing the company's strategic plan until they can do their day-to-day work with consistency and quality, that means they don't yet have a realistic sense of performance management.

Staying loose on performance objectives so that multiple

teams can shuttle their way to full empowerment is a desirable goal, even if it's not always practical. When the organization's empowerment plans are strategic and uniformity is important, say for consistent customer service or to meet lowered headcount targets, it becomes critical for teams to move in a coordinated fashion, adding new tasks and clarifying roles with management direction and involvement.

The manager in one company learned the importance of managing team performance after a year of letting teams feel their way. At that point, some teams had made significant progress while others floundered, still uncertain of their mandate and expectations. To help lagging teams build a structure that enabled them to move ahead, the steering committee drafted job descriptions that clearly laid out duties and responsibilities in each of several key areas, including Quality, Team Function, Administration, Safety and Housekeeping, Production, and Tools and Materials.

The following list gives some idea of the level of detail required to ensure that the basics get done. This example shows how Team Function—a category that encompassed such things as meetings, self-management, and communications—was defined by a set of clear guidelines.

Team Function: Example
- Teams will meet weekly other than during the meal break (not to exceed 45-60 minutes) to address team duties and problem solving. An approved agenda and structured meeting format are required. Meeting roles will rotate.
- Teams will monitor performance against established goals for attendance, quality, safety, and job performance.
- Teams will identify and problem-solve any issues that keep them from meeting their goals.
- Teams will address and counsel any team member whose performance or conduct (such as attendance, quality, safety, work habits, etc.) violates company rules or hampers the smooth function of the team.
- Teams will document any such counseling.
- Teams will communicate in writing all such unresolved

issues to appropriate management personnel for direction and support.

In addition, the steering committee drafted a detailed set of team leader job duties to support each of those functional areas. Without clear goals, teams may fail to grasp the principle of mastery as it concerns the gradual acquisition of tasks.

Optimism Tempered by Realism

Smart Managing

Be optimistic but realistic—from the beginning. That's tough, especially when everybody is so enthusiastic and ambitious.

But it's smart to set realistic expectations. You'll make about the same progress as if you'd set higher expectations, but you get a greater feeling of success exceeding expectations than just meeting them. That feeling can really help keep your enthusiasm and ambition alive and growing.

If this all sounds a bit draconian, consider the consequences of failing to ensure a smooth transition from basic to sophisticated tasks. Too many teams have leapt ahead, only to find themselves in uncharted waters, out of their depth and without a compass. The results of this have been frustration, poor performance, and, ultimately, dissolution of the empowerment vision. A good maxim of empowerment is that it's always easier to loosen up than tighten up. Power delegated all at once is more difficult to take back than when it's given in phases and connected to performance and achievement.

Make the New Tasks Work as Flawlessly as the Basic Ones

As levels of empowerment build up, the speed of the process increases. The problem is not in getting teams to take responsibility for complex organizational communications, but in getting them to do their timekeeping or basic office management.

As you can see in Figure 11-2, team development is a matter of personal development as well. Unless a team member gets some positive feedback from the team when entering the picture, he or she will be reluctant to pair up, plan, or take action. Moving through this process for one empowerment

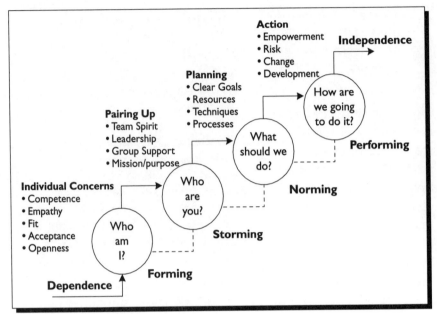

Figure 11-2. Who am I and who are you?

task makes it easier to move through it for subsequent tasks, because the personal relationships—including trust and cooperation—will have been established.

The real benefit of the "Who Am I and Who Are You?" concept is that once you have moved from isolation and individuality to team performance, even on a simple task, the return is simpler and faster.

One of the best ways to begin is with a "demonstration activity." For a demonstration activity, you select a project or empowerment task that interests the team and that the team is willing to take on. In selecting a demonstration activity, take some of the following criteria into consideration.

The project or task:
- Fits your *cultures* and the *personalities* of your team members.
- Is seen by all as *important* and *needing improvement*.
- Is relatively *simple* and *easy* to implement.
- Will show *quick results*.
- Can be *measured* and *tracked*.

In selecting initial empowerment tasks, follow these guidelines to provide a firm foundation for building flawless performance:

1. Move from simple to more complex tasks.
2. Begin with tasks that are already going well.
3. Start with tasks involving things, rather than people.
4. Document the delegation, using an empowerment plan.

Complexity The opposite of simplicity. But complexity may be also the effect of cumulative simplicity.

Sometimes a thing may be simple—but only from each of a number of perspectives. When you have to consider all those perspectives, a simple thing suddenly becomes complex.

There's an old saying that applies well here: "You think because you understand 'one' you must understand 'two' because one and one make two. But you must also understand 'and.'"

When you bring things together, that "and" moves you from the simplicity of one to the complexity of two ... or usually many more.

Move from simple to more complex tasks. This may seem a bit obvious, but it's worth a moment to consider the complexity hidden in the most elementary task. Complexity is not confined to some mechanical operation, body of knowledge, or technical sophistication; it may involve the use of judgment and decision making.

For example, a restaurant committed to customer service, as part of an overall empowerment plan, encouraged its servers to make decisions about whether or not to offer coupons for free dinners, appetizers, or desserts to patrons who voiced a complaint about their dinners. Before long, coupons were flowing freely as the servers discovered that they could increase their tips by passing out a coupon for a free meal. The servers weren't out to undermine the restaurant, of course; they just didn't understand the big picture, the reasons behind the coupons. No limits were put on their use of the coupons, no written guidelines, and no process for monitoring the effect of the coupons on business.

You can use the Team Empowerment Planning Worksheet (described later) to quickly distinguish between simple and complex tasks.

Begin with tasks that are already going well. Again, this may seem obvious. But enthusiasm and ambition may move you to overlook the obvious.

One of the first empowerment tasks we attempted in a large rehabilitation hospital with a team of social workers was to turn over the task of determining how a relatively small lump sum of outside training and education money would be spent. This job had previously been done by the team's director, a well-intentioned, thoughtful woman who was mercilessly criticized by the group for her decisions in this area.

At first the team was happy with the new arrangement, but within weeks members were back to their old disputes over who went where when. They couldn't overcome the history: the disposition of their limited training funds had become, over the years, a discretionary perk and was fraught with controversy.

For this group, a better empowerment choice would have been a task that may seem more complex—organizing detailed case management meetings. Although this was the director's responsibility, the case management sessions were already being handled by the case workers. The director's role in these meetings had become secondary, and she was happy to be free from her obligation to superintend a process in which she had no responsibilities.

The lesson to be learned from this is that most teams have already taken on tasks they are comfortable with. You can turn these tasks into empowered delegations in the space of a single team meeting with ease. You don't need to revisit them frequently to troubleshoot, and the manager won't have to worry whether the work gets done.

The difference between just leaving things as they are and formalizing the process can be significant. When you re-engineer the task to be taken over by the team, you increase the structure, formulate an action plan, adopt measurement standards, and set up a standard operating procedure. This structure is put in writing and used to train new team members. Since the process is documented, it's less open to change and misinterpretation than if it depended on oral transmission.

Start with tasks involving things, rather than people.
Vacation planning, holiday scheduling, overtime allocation,
telephone coverage, and attendance monitoring—all are common tasks that involve minimal record keeping. So they
should be a snap for any team. Right?

Maybe. But when it comes to personal time, attendance,
and other issues with strong personal considerations, history
tends to repeat itself. When team members have worked well
together providing for shift or vacation coverage with few complaints or hurt feelings, they may be able to manage their own
schedule. But when issues like these have been the source of
problems that only the supervisor could handle, it's asking for
trouble to lay this kind of
high-impact, high-emo-
tion decision making on
the team.

Unless the team
members are acquainted
with the tools of conflict
management, they'll get
into trouble when the first
unanticipated conflict
arises. Since most people
can't work together in the

> ### Give the Reasons
> When you set boundaries,
> state the reasons for each
> boundary. There are two advantages to
> doing this.
>   First, if your employees understand
> why a boundary exists, they're more
> likely to respect it. Second, sharing your
> reasons is a form of empowerment:
> you're involving your employees in the
> thinking behind your decision.

presence of open conflict and confrontation, they'll avoid the
issues, they'll accommodate, and they'll hide resentments for a
while, but they'll later surface in full bloom.

Rather than risk this scenario, managers would be wise to
go with what already works well or to identify, possibly with the
help of the team, some of the more routine duties that no
longer need management involvement. These duties vary by
industry, but include logging customer complaints, maintaining
or updating status boards, gathering inventory figures or
month-end closing numbers, compiling budget information,
and timekeeping for work orders. When delegated as empowerment tasks, these routine duties become good demonstration
activities that give the team confidence and assure management that the process is working.

Team Empowerment Planning Worksheet

1. **Describe the Empowerment Task.**
   This is an operational definition of the task with examples.

2. **Map the Current Process.**
   This is a detailed description of how the task is currently handled. It can be done in words or with a flow chart.

3. **Set Short- and Long-Term Goals.**
   The purpose of setting short-term goals is to get the process started. Usually short-term goals are set for a first team meeting or a date when the team will start taking over the new task. Longer-term goals may involve holding the team accountable for results.

4. **Determine Key Roles.**
   Key roles are usually roles played by managers, the team leader, and the team members. In a complex delegation, role responsibility may be skewed toward management at first, since managers may want to retain planning and organization. Later on, role responsibility should move to the team leader and the team. In a simple delegation, managers may have little or no role.

5. **Set Task Boundaries.**
   Boundary-setting gauges the outer limits of the team's authority. It's as important for the team to know what it can't do as what it can do. Such things as legal requirements, policy restrictions, and negotiated agreements are usually set out of bounds.

6. **Develop a New Standard Operating Procedure (SOP).**
   An SOP is a way of documenting a team duty, to ensure consistent performance and to transfer the duties to new team members. Many jobs already have SOPs, in the form of training or policy manuals, but it's important to document new tasks so that team members understand them and take them seriously.

Figure 11-3. Team empowerment planning worksheet

Document the delegation, using an empowerment plan. An empowerment plan is no more than a system for documenting how the new task will be transferred from management control to team control. This tool—the Team Empowerment Planning Worksheet in Figure 11-3—is a detailed action plan that specifies what, when, who, and how much.

One method of creating this action plan requires managers and team members to think through the delegation and complete a worksheet that considers such things as goals, boundaries, and standard operating procedures.

Repeat, ad Infinitum

The real benefits of empowerment are seldom felt early in the process. Initially, it's a matter of investing in hiring the right people, training them, and working closely with them long enough to get them comfortable with the range of management duties they're expected to perform. The payoff comes later on when, with little supervision, they're able to take a task and, using this system, make it part of their work.

Manager's Checklist for Chapter 11

❑ Empowerment is not a natural process. Think through the process, consider potential problems, ask a few hard questions, and consider how employees might receive and interpret your goals.

❑ Understand and abide by the five principles for more effective empowerment.

❑ Think of empowerment as a process for helping the *right people* at the *right levels* make the *right decisions* for the *right reasons*. That definition raises the questions that you need to answer.

Evaluating Your Team

This chapter is the shortest of all. It consists of several instruments that you can use to evaluate your team or teams. More important, however, I hope it inspires you.

How do you evaluate your team? That depends primarily on the goals you set when you began planning your team approach.

Review those goals. (They should be posted on your office wall and in prominent places around your work area.) How well have you and your teams done? What progress have you made? What achievements should you celebrate? In which areas do you most need to improve?

What Are Your Team Performance Problems?

We'll start with a simple self-audit, adapted from an audit developed by James H. Folsom of The Wings Group, editor of *TeamZene*. Answer "Yes" or "No" to the following questions. Distribute copies of these questions to your team members and ask them to do the same—anonymously, of course, perhaps at the end of a team meeting.

1. Do the team members understand the team purpose, mission, and goals?

2. Have the team members had input into developing the purpose, mission, and goals?
3. Do the team members share a common approach and commitment to their purpose?
4. Do the team members feel they can achieve their purpose with the support and resources provided?
5. Has the team developed its own operating norms and team process?
6. Are members frequently missing from meetings and/or new members added?
7. Does the team include an "authority figure" who "pulls rank" on the rest of the team?
8. Will several of the team members be negatively impacted by the expected outcome?
9. Do any members try to assume any roles beyond the ones assigned?
10. Are the team members expected to do both their "regular" work and the work of the team?

Any "No" answers to the first five questions or "Yes" answers to the last five questions point to problems. Problems revealed by any of the first five questions should become the focus of a team meeting, as soon as possible. Problems revealed by the last five are up to you, as manager and coach.

Problems with the issue raised in question 10 may be normal and inevitable, at least until the team has been developing for a while. But you should probably find ways to ease your expectations, so your employees don't feel burdened by two loads and pulled in two directions.

Questions 6 through 9 call for a follow-up survey. Distribute copies of a questionnaire consisting of those four questions, each followed by the simple question, "Who?" Again, it's essential to have your team members do the survey anonymously.

Once you know which of your team members are identified by their teammates as the reasons for "Yes" answers to questions 6 through 9, you've got a big and critical assignment as their coach.

How Effective Is Your Team?

You should regularly assess your team in terms of your conceptual team behaviors. Those are the guidelines or expectations that you established in forming your team. They would generally include such behaviors as the following:

- The team acts in terms of its purpose, mission, and goals.
- The team uses the team process and adheres to team norms in making any decisions.
- Team members are committed to cooperation and collaboration.
- The team has defined its measures of success.
- The team monitors its performance according to its measures of success.
- Team members rotate in the roles of meeting leader, facilitator, scribe, and note-taker.
- Team members use direct dealing to resolve conflicts.
- Team members participate actively in meetings.

Once you've got your conceptual team behaviors in writing, you can construct an appropriate survey instrument.

For each behavior, set up a four-point Likert scale, from 1 (ineffective) to 4 (effective). Then, customize the scale for each behavior, to indicate to your team members what the terms "ineffective" and "effective" mean for that specific behavior.

Using our list of common behaviors as an example, your instrument might look like the one partially depicted in Figure 12-1.

Distribute copies of your team survey among your team members, and ask them to each rate the behaviors listed, as truthfully as possible. (Yes,

Likert scale A rating using several numbers, usually between four and seven. The fewer numbers you use, the less accurate your results. But the more you use, the more complicated and time-consuming you make your rating instrument.

Some testing experts recommend that the scale use an even number of points, because with an odd number people may naturally choose the middle point, the easiest way.

Rate the team for each of these behaviors

1. The team acts in terms of its purpose, mission, and goals.

   rarely   1   2   3   4   usually

2. The team uses the team process and adheres to team norms in making any decisions.

   rarely   1   2   3   4   usually

3. Team members are committed to cooperation and collaboration.

   some,   1   2   3   4   most,
   sometimes   generally

4. The team has defined its measures of success.

   vaguely   1   2   3   4   clearly

5. The team monitors its performance according to its measures of success.

   somewhat   1   2   3   4   absolutely

6. Team members rotate in the roles of meeting leader, facilitator, scribe, and note-taker.

   sporadically   1   2   3   4   regularly

7. Team members use direct dealing to resolve conflicts.

   poorly   1   2   3   4   successfully

8. Team members participate actively in meetings.

   some,   1   2   3   4   most,
   sometimes   generally

Figure 12-1. Team effectiveness survey

once again, this assessment should be done anonymously. In an ideal work environment, you could conduct an open assessment during a team meeting. Maybe you could add that goal to your list, as a true test for your team?)

Take the completed assessment forms and calculate the average of all the ratings for each conceptual behavior. Then you know where to focus your attention. You should also note any extreme rating splits—1s and 4s. After all, whether the ratings are all 2s and 3s or all 1s and 4s, your averages could be about the same—but those ratings would certainly reflect different feelings about those behaviors! Extreme rating splits reveal opinion gaps among team members. You'll want to work on closing those gaps or you'll risk leaving some members behind, even though the team might be doing very well.

How Good Are the Members of the Team?

Asking your team members to evaluate the team leads naturally to asking them to evaluate each other. But first make sure they're comfortable with evaluating the team; peer review can be difficult.

To develop an instrument, you start with your expectations. What do you and the team members expect from each member of your team? Then, you create a matrix, listing those expectations down the side, with a Likert scale beside each, and listing your team members across the top. (Yes, that means that every team member will also be evaluating himself or herself. That provides a little "reality check.")

Your instrument might look something like the team peer review in Figure 12-2. I've listed eight expectations in five categories; you'll likely have at least double that. Be specific: avoid global statements such as "Communicates appropriately" or "Shows team spirit."

Of course, your team will want to change its peer review instrument as the situation changes. It's not something to etch into stone.

The first few times you conduct peer evaluations, it may be best for you to score the results yourself. Then, when your team members become more comfortable with the process, you can appoint somebody to handle that task, rotating it among the members as you rotate the responsibilities of meeting leader, facilitator, scribe, and note-taker.

Scoring the results is simple. Create a form based on your peer review instrument, such as shown in Figure 12-3. For each team member, average the ratings received from his or her teammates, keeping each member's self-evaluation ratings separate. Finally, calculate the team average for each expectation.

Team Members:	Mary	Julio	Anthony	Renée	Peggy	Marc
Participation						
Takes active part in team activities.	____	____	____	____	____	____
Communication						
Expresses his or her opinion openly.	____	____	____	____	____	____
Expresses his or her opinion clearly.	____	____	____	____	____	____
Listens to the opinions of others.	____	____	____	____	____	____
Cooperation						
Helps teammates when needed.	____	____	____	____	____	____
Team Spirit						
Acts in the best interests of the team.	____	____	____	____	____	____
Uses direct dealing to resolve problems.	____	____	____	____	____	____
Innovation						
Focuses on finding ways to improve.	____	____	____	____	____	____

Figure 12-2. Team peer review

Provide each team member with his or her results. (Put a copy in each member's files as well.) It's generally best not to distribute the results during a meeting. But for at least the first few reviews, you may want to schedule time during a meeting to discuss how to improve the results.

Peer reviews are difficult, but they make sense for at least four reasons:

- Teamwork depends on the performance of every member of the team, so every member should be evaluated individually.
- Evaluation of team members shouldn't be your responsibility alone, since you're not going to be everywhere to know everything about everybody.
- Team members should develop their critical abilities; peer evaluations provide a good means of developing those abilities.
- Team members who have experience evaluating each other will better appreciate the tough evaluations required of managers.

These results show how your teammates have evaluated your performance on the team, using the following scale: 1=rarely, 2=sometimes, 3=usually, 4=always

Name _____   **Date** _____

	Team Score	Self Score	Team Average
Participation			
Takes active part in team activities.	____	____	____
Communication			
Expresses his or her opinion openly.	____	____	____
Expresses his or her opinion clearly.	____	____	____
Listens to the opinions of others.	____	____	____
Cooperation			
Helps teammates when needed.	____	____	____
Team Spirit			
Acts in the best interests of the team.	____	____	____
Uses direct dealing to resolve problems.	____	____	____
Innovation			
Focuses on finding ways to improve.	____	____	____

Figure 12-3. Team peer review results

How Else Can You Evaluate Your Team?

I hope that question is on your mind at this point. And the answer is (drum roll) ... it's up to you and your team.

For any of your team activities—meetings, projects, assignments, and general collaboration—or any other aspects of working as a team—team spirit, leadership, and even the manager!—you can develop some form of assessment. Chapter 8 offered some examples. I'll give two more here. Then you can discuss evaluation during your next team meeting.

Meetings

How good are your meetings? As I stressed in Chapter 8, meetings are a vital team activity. So you might try a two-minute check every time you meet.

Simply end each meeting by having the meeting leader pass around 3 x 5 or 4 x 6 index cards, one to each member. Then ask three basic, open-ended questions:

1. What did you like most about this meeting?
2. What did you like least about this meeting?
3. How could we have had a better meeting?

Sure, it's not a formal, detailed assessment. But sometimes a "gut check" can reveal a lot. And you can always ask more specific questions, particularly as you identify persistent problem areas.

In *The Team Handbook*, Peter R. Scholtes and associates suggest assessing meetings with Likert scales, asking members to rate the meeting on such continua as "Wonderful-Lousy," "Very focused-Rambling," and "Energetic-Lethargic." It takes a little more time to prepare this sort of assessment form, but you can focus on areas you consider problematic.

Manager

Here's another example of a do-it-yourself assessment, for something a little closer to home. How good are you as a team manager? That's a very important question—especially if it makes you feel uncomfortable.

Act on Your Evaluations

CAUTION!

What's worse than not evaluating? Not acting on what your evaluations reveal. Sometimes it's almost as bad to take action, but fail to communicate that action.

If you find big problems that involve the whole team, address them at a team meeting. If the problems concern certain members of the team, handle them yourself, by coaching the individuals, one on one. The other members of the team should know by the results that you've taken action to solve the problems.

If you find little problems that don't involve individual members, simply take care of them yourself or—usually better—assign members of the team to handle them. Either way, it's appropriate to report on your actions at a team meeting.

When Ed Koch was mayor of New York, he'd frequently ask people on the streets a simple question, "How am I doing?" That question took guts.

Every manager should ask that question, whenever and wherever possible. Of course, you should generally focus that big question to make it more effective.

What do you expect of yourself as manager? What goals have you set for your performance? What qualities are crucial to your role as team manager? What behaviors are essential?

Draw up a list and attach a Likert scale to each item. Ask your team members to evaluate you (anonymously).

Yes, it takes guts to ask, "How am I doing?" But that's a vital part of being a leader.

Manager's Checklist for Chapter 12

❑ Evaluation is essential. You need to measure the progress you've made toward your goals and determine the areas in which you most need to improve.

❑ Evaluation is dangerous. You need to be sensitive any time you're assessing people, but especially for tasks that are new to them—and most particularly when those tasks involve collaboration.

❑ Evaluate whatever matters most to you. The evaluation should be done by every member of the team, not just by you.

Index

A

Accountability, 101

B

Bach, Richard, 70
Bennis, Warren, 70
Blanchard, Kenneth, 70
Bounds, Gregory M., 111, 147
Brainstorming, 60, 122-24, 125
Business strategy
  and advanced manufacturing
    technologies, 36, 37, 38
  checklist for, 42
  complexity criteria for, 38
  driving forces for, 31-33
  function to process, 34-35
  guidelines for, 41-42
  judgment criteria for, 38
  labor-intensive criteria for, 39
  and people readiness, 39-40,
    41
  and quality management, 35
  reasons for, 34-36, 37, 38, 41
  reorganizing and downsizing,
    35-36
  restraining forces against,
    31-33
  shared responsibility criteria
    for, 39
  and skills needed, 33

  socio-technical analysis for,
    33
  and technology reasons, 34
  work, appropriateness of,
    37-39, 41

C

Changes, coping with
  amount of, 166
  checklist for, 169
  control, loss of, 165
  doubts about the past, 166
  failure, fear of, 166
  managing effectively, 166-69
  resentments, past, 166
  resistance, causes, 165-66
  ripple effects, 166, 167
  risks, real, 166
  surprise, 165
  uncertainty, 165
  work, increasing, 166
Coaching
  assignments, 138-40
  and awards and recognition,
    147
  basics of, 130-31
  checklist for, 149
  and coercive power, 138
  competence, confidence, and
    comfort zone, 135

and connection power, 138
defined, 129-30
desired performance, demon-
    strating, 132
from a distance, 144-45, 146
by example, 148
expectations, raising, 135-36
and expert power, 138
facilitators, 111-12, 114-15,
    142-43
feedback, providing, 134, 135
follow-up, 132-33
and high-output questions,
    146
job performance, 131-36
leaders, 137-44
meeting leaders, 111, 113-16,
    142-43
for meetings, 140-44
note-takers, 112-13, 115,
    143
performance, 135-36
and personal power, 138
players as coaches, 145-46
and position power, 137
and positive atmosphere, 132
and praise, 133
for problems, 133-34
and recognition, 146-48
and resource power, 138
and reward power, 138
scribes, 112, 115, 143
skills, training, 131
success and failure, as
    companions, 134
team players, 136-37
and trust and patience, 138-
    40
Communication, 10-11

Complexity, 183
Conflicts, coping with
    accommodating style, 162-63
    avoiding style, 161-62
    barriers to resolving, 153-54
    body language, 159
    checklist for, 169
    climate for resolving, 150-51
    collaborating style, 164-65
    by common ground,
        establishing, 153
    confrontation, fear of, 153
    confronting style, 163-64
    consequences, concern for,
        154
    direct dealing technique, 96,
        151-54, 158-59
    formal process, lack of, 154
    in forming phase, 81, 83, 85,
        159-60
    by impact of problems,
        explaining, 152
    information, lack of, 154
    by interest in others' ideas,
        153
    by listening to others' point of
        view, 152
    in norming phase, 82, 83, 85,
        160
    Observer Feedback Form,
        157
    people, handling conflict,
        160-65
    in performing phase, 82, 83,
        85, 160
    Planning Guide, 156
    power levels, 153
    by problems statements, in
        behavioral terms, 152

by reducing occurrences of,
159-65
reflecting technique, 155-58,
159
skills, lack of, 154
sources of, 159
in storming phase, 81-82, 83,
160
support, lack of, 153
third party, role, 154-55
Consensus, 59
Corporate Cultures (Deal and
Kennedy), 110
Culture for teamwork
business today, 22-23, 24
checklist for, 30
failure, example, 25-26
and functions of a team,
21-22
high-performance work
teams, 20, 21
and old management, 26-28
overview, 19-22
preparation for, 28
readiness for, 24-30
for self-directed teams, 20,
21, 23-24, 25
for social functions, 22
teams, defined, 3-8, 21
for technical functions, 22
for traditional management
functions, 22
from traditional to self-
directed, 23-24

D
Deal, Terrence, 110
Deeprose, Donna, 147
Deming Prize, 101

Direct dealing technique, 96,
151-54, 158-59
Dynamics of teams
blaming managers for everything, 90-91
checklist for, 99
"circle of influence," 85-86
communications, 94-96
"direct dealing," 96, 151-54,
158-59
force-rank, 96, 97
in forming, "honeymoon"
phase, 81, 83, 85, 159-60
and the genius, 93
in norming, "reality strikes"
phase, 82, 83, 85, 160
and the overemployed, 94
peer pressure within, 93-94
performance problems, 96-99
in performing, "synergy"
phase, 82, 83, 85, 160
problems, common, 82-99
quitting at first obstacle,
89-90
resistance to changing work
roles, 91-93
results focus, ignoring
process, 88-89
and Silent Sams, 93-94
and the steward, 94
in storming, "post-honey-
moon" phase, 81-82, 83,
85, 160
too much too soon, 86-87
and the underemployed, 94
unrealistic expectations,
coping with, 85-86
work styles, differences in,
87-88

E

Effort, 127

Effort-Impact Action Planning, 122, 125-28

Empowerment, applied
adding new tasks when previous tasks are mastered, 179-81
beginning with tasks that are going well, 183-84
boundaries, and reasons for, 185
checklist for, 187
and complexity, 183
defined, 172, 175
"demonstration activities," 182
doing the basics first, 175-76
handoff of responsibilities, 178
learning to do things flawlessly, 177-79
making the new tasks work as flawlessly as the basic ones, 181-87
optimism and realism, 181
planning too little and expecting too much, 172-73
principles for, 174-87
problems with, examples, 170-72
"professional cynics," 177
repeating, ad infinitum, 187
and results, 172
schedule for, 178-79
and simple to complex, 183
starting tasks involving things rather than people, 184-85

Team Empowerment Planning Worksheet, 185-87
"Who Am I and Who Are You?" Concept, 181-82
(see also Business strategy; Changes, coping with; Coaching; Conflicts, coping with; Culture for teamwork; Dynamics of teams; Evaluation; Leadership; Meetings, conducting; Problems and reasons why; Questions, before starting; Teams; Vision and values)

Evaluation
acting on your evaluations, 195
checklist for, 196
of effectiveness, 190-92
Likert scale, use of, 190
of manager, 195-96
of meetings, 194-95
of members, 192-94
of performance problems, 188-89
using peer reviews, 192-94

F

Facilitators, 111-12, 114-15, 142-43
Florida Power and Light, 101
Folsom, James H., 188
Force-rank, 96, 97
Forming: "honeymoon" phase, 81, 83, 85, 159-60
Franklin, Benjamin, 136

G

Goldsmith, Oliver, 148

H
Harvard University, 102-3
High-performance work teams, 20-21

I
Illusions (Bach), 70
Impact, 127
In Search of Excellence (Peters and Waterman), 70

K
Kennedy, Allan, 110
Klein, Janice, 102-3
Koch, Ed, 195-96
Kotter, John, 70

L
Leaders: The Strategies For Taking Charge (Nanus), 70
Leadership
    from within, 78-79
    and accountability, 101
    by advising on problem or opportunity selection, 102, 105
    by assisting in implementation, 102, 106-7
    and assumptions, 100-101
    and "black boxes," 107
    checklist for, 108
    by coaching on problem solving, 102, 106
    by coordinating team activities, 102, 104-5
    and power bases, 103-4
    by providing recognition, 102, 107-8
    by providing resources, 102, 105-6

questions, before starting, 13-14
    responsibility, as opportunity, 108
    self-analysis of, 104-8
    using coercive power, 103-4
    using connection power, 104
    using expert power, 103
    using personal power, 103
    using position power, 103
    using resource power, 103
    using reward power, 103
Leadership Factor, The (Kotter), 70
Likert scale, use of, 190
Lowe's Companies, 99

M
McGregor, Douglas, 15
Meeting leaders, 111, 113-16, 142-43
Meetings, conducting
    action plans, 127-28
    affinity diagrams, 124
    and anger, 119-20
    and bogging, 111
    brainstorming, 122-24, 125
    checklist for, 128
    and clogging, 111
    coaching for, 140-44
    and commitment, lack of, 119
    and compromise, 117
    and disrupters, 118
    effort, 127
    Effort-Impact Action Planning, 122, 125-28
    evaluating, 194-95
    facilitators, 111-12, 114-15, 142-43

and flogging, 111
and focus, lack of, 118
and fogging, 111
and follow-up, 116
and frogging, 111
green lighting, 125
guidelines for, 113-16
and hogging, 111
and idea sharing, 116
impact, 127
and late arrivals, 120
and listening, 116-17
meeting leaders, 111, 113-16,
    142-43
and negative attitudes, 117-18
norms, developing, 116-17
note-takers, 112-13, 115,
    143
and preliminaries, 114
preparation for, 114
problem-solving techniques,
    117-28
problems with, 109-10, 111
responsibility, taking, 117
and role sharing, 113
and roles of, 110-13
scribes, 112, 115, 143
and silence, 118-19
Situation-Target-Options-Plan
    (STOP), 121-22
Specific, Measurable, Agreed
    Upon, Reachable, Time-
    Bound (SMART) goals,
    122, 124-25
Mirroring, 155-58, 159
Mission statements, 73-74
    (*see also* Vision and values)
MIT robot experiment, 174

N
Nanus, Burt, 70
Norming: "reality strikes" phase,
    82, 83, 85, 160
Note-takers, 112-13, 115, 143

O
One-Minute Manager, The
    (Blanchard), 70

P
Performing: "synergy" phase,
    82, 83, 85, 160
Peters, Tom, 70
Problems and reasons why
    action items, 63-64
    avoiding, tips for, 54-57
    the bait-and-switch, 47-48
    "boundary diagrams," 56-57
    brainstorming, 60, 122-24,
        125
    and business plans, 55
    checklist for, 66
    consensus, 59
    the dump, 45-47
    and expectations, 56-57
    during experimentation, 60
    focus groups, 46
    future, describing (exercise),
        50
    during learning, 58
    and mistakes, imagining, 52
    optimism and realism,
        balance of, 45
    read my mind, 48-51
    and resources, 55-56
    and roles, defining, 56
    during sharing and growing,
        62

during strategy development, 59

structured responsibility hand-offs, 48

team development, strategy for, 57-66

during testing and evaluation, 61

try it—you'll like it, 52-54

and visioning, 51

yes, but, 51-52

(*see also* Mission statements; Vision and values)

Q

Questions, before starting
about compensation, 16, 17

about evaluating progress in changing environments, 12-13

about evaluation, individual and team, 14-16

about expectations, 11-13

about leadership, 13-14

about organizational impacts of teams, 17-18

about people in teams, 7-8

about place in organizational structure, 4-5

about plan or structure, 6-7

about power, responsibilities, authority, 5-6

about purpose, 3-4

about resources for training and development, 16-17

about roles, 13-14

about targets and goals, 12, 13

checklist for, 18

and communication, 10-11

and failure, reasons for, 2-3

and focused thinking, 10

and honesty, 18

and organization's characteristics, 5

reasons for teams, 8-9

resistance to teams, 1-2

and synergy, 9

teams, defined, 3-8, 21

Theory X & Y managers, 15

and trinkets, 17

and trust-based relationships, 11

where to implement, 9-11

R

Recognition, 102, 107-8, 146-48

Reflecting, 155-58, 159

S

Scholtes, Peter R., 168, 195

Scribes, 112, 115, 143

Self-directed teams, 20, 21, 23-24, 25

Shames, Lawrence, 134

Situation-Target-Options-Plan (STOP), 121-22

Socio-technical analysis, 33

Specific, Measurable, Agreed Upon, Reachable, Time-Bound (SMART) goals, 122, 124-25

Storming: "post-honeymoon" phase, 81-82, 83, 85, 160

Strategy, 57-66, 74-78

(*see also* Business strategy)

Supervision (Bounds and Woods), 111, 147

Synergy, 9, 82, 83, 85, 160

T

Team Coach, The (Deeprose), 147

Team Handbook, The (Scholtes), 168, 195

Teams, 3-8, 21
(*see also* Business strategy; Changes, coping with; Coaching; Conflicts, coping with; Culture for teamwork; Empowerment, applied; Dynamics of teams; Evaluation; Leadership; Meetings, conducting; Problems and reasons why; Questions, before starting; Vision and values)

TeamZene (Folsom), 188

Third Wave (Toffler), 70

Toffler, Alvin, 70

V

Vision and values
analytic approach to, 71-72
benchmarking approach to, 72-73
checklist for, 79-80
creating, 69-73
difficulties, 75-76
evaluation, continuous, 77
"5 Ws and 1H" (who, what, when, were, why, how), 72
focusing on successes, 77-78
goals, setting, 76
importance of, 67-68
intuitive approach to, 71
leadership from within, 78-79
mission statements, 73-74
plans, putting to work, 77
progress measurement, 75
rewarding achievements, 78
strategy for success, 74-78
support for, building, 77
tactics and actions, deciding on, 76
values, defined, 68-69
visioning principles, 73
visions, defined, 68-69
(*see also* Problems and reasons why)

W

Wings Group, The, 188

Woods, John A., 111, 147